Holt Spanish

Exploratory Guide

For use with materials from
¡Ven conmigo!®, Level 1,
or
Adelante, Level 1A, and
En camino, Level 1B

HOLT, RINEHART AND WINSTON

A Harcourt Classroom Education Company

Austin · New York · Orlando · Atlanta · San Francisco · Boston · Dallas · Toronto · London

Contributing Writers:

Rachel Norwood

Rachel Pooley

Consultant and Contributing Writer:

JoAnne Wilson

Reviewers:

Richard Lindley

Mayanne Wright

PHOTO/ART CREDITS
Abbreviations as follows: (t) top, (b) bottom, (l) left, (r) right, (c) center.
Photo Credits
Front Cover: John Langford/HRW Photo; Page v, John Langford/HRW Photo; 80 (c), Superstock;
96 (all), Marty Granger/Edge Productions/HRW; 108 (all), Marty Granger/Edge Productions/HRW.
Art Credits
All art, unless otherwise noted, contributed by Holt, Rinehart & Winston.

Page 2, MapQuest.com; 4, Elizabeth Brandt; 11, MapQuest.com; 12, Elizabeth Brandt; 14 (t, b), Edson
Campos; 14 (c), Precision Graphics; 16, Edson Campos; 18, Edson Campos; 24 (t), Edson Campos;
24 (c), Precision Graphics; 28, Michael Morrow Design; 32, Holly Cooper; 35, Holly Cooper; 36, Holly
Cooper; 38, Edson Campos; 40, Yves Larvor; 44, Edson Campos; 47, Edson Campos; 48, Edson Campos;
56, Elizabeth Brandt; 59, Bethann Thornburgh; 88, Meryl Henderson; 88, Edson Campos; 92, Jocelyne
Bouchard; 96, Meryl Henderson; 96, Edson Campos.

Printed in the United States of America

ISBN 0-03-065903-5

1 2 3 4 5 6 7   066   05 04 03 02 01

Contents

To the Teacher

The *Holt Spanish Exploratory Guide* is designed to help you create interest in language learning in younger students. It provides detailed lesson plans, activity suggestions, and review and assessment options for a full-fledged Exploratory Spanish Course. On pages vi–viii you will find a brief introduction to the philosophy behind exploratory education and some suggestions on how to maximize this learning opportunity for students.

Each of the nine units in this book includes vocabulary and cultural information that students will find interesting and relevant to their daily lives. Each unit is theme-based and is built around materials from the Holt Spanish program. You can use *Adelante* and *En camino* resources, or you can build your course with parallel resources from *¡Ven conmigo!* Level 1. Many of the ancillaries available with **Holt Spanish**—including the *Teaching Transparencies,* the *Audio Program,* the *Interactive CD-ROM Tutor,* the *DVD Tutor,* and the *Video Program*—readily lend themselves to use in an exploratory setting.

A unit-by-unit list of any additional materials needed precedes Unit 1. The lesson plans in this Exploratory Guide provide specific suggestions on how to use these resources to construct an effective, motivational, and culturally rich exploratory program.

Content of the Exploratory Guide

This guide contains nine thematic units, each designed to be completed in a five-day school week. Units 1–3 should be done in sequence to help students develop a foundation of basic concepts and core vocabulary. Units 4–9 can be done in any order, which allows you to respond readily to the particular needs and interests of students. This also enables you to tailor the exploratory course to the amount of time allotted.

For a six-week course you can present Units 1–3 plus any other three units desired. For a nine-week course you can present Units 1–3, and then the remaining six units in any order. To accommodate a twelve-week course, you may choose to extend some units using the suggestions in the Additional Practice section found at the end of each lesson.

Unit Structure

Each unit provides four detailed daily lesson plans, a vocabulary list, a page with review and assessment options, and a two-page written assessment instrument, **¡Ya lo sé!** *(I know this!).* All four lesson plans begin with a list of Holt Spanish resources available to present and reinforce the material. The resources have been carefully selected to support exploratory level instruction. Additional materials required, such as index cards, tape, and scissors, are also listed at the beginning of the lesson. Lesson plans are structured in a clear-cut, organized manner. Each lesson includes a motivating activity, cultural information, sequential teaching activities, and an additional practice section, as well as a project and a closing activity. The teaching suggestions are designed to give you numerous age-appropriate teaching options. Since the goal of exploratory courses is to create interest in language learning, these suggestions provide ideas for presenting and practicing the material in the most creative, fun ways possible. The lessons incorporate games, songs, TPR activities, projects, and other hands-on activities. In addition, each lesson plan is accompanied by an activity master that gives students a chance to practice the targeted material on their own.

At the end of each unit, the Review and Assessment page gives you suggestions for review activities, a project that reinforces and demonstrates student knowledge of unit vocabulary, and in-class oral assessment suggestions. The **¡Ya lo sé!** activity master provides students with a chance to demonstrate in writing what they have learned. This activity master can be used to evaluate student progress and to determine if there is a need to provide further practice of the material.

Exploring Language
Foreign Language Exploratory Classes

By Jo Anne Wilson

The placement of an Exploratory class at the beginning of middle school opens the door to language learning early. Early exploration leads to early opportunity to begin a skills-based program, thus making longer language sequences possible.

Foreign language educators have long known that learning a second language is best done at a young age. The Standards for Foreign Language Learning K–12 advocate longer language sequences based on an early start and an extended period of study. Both of these factors have led to a proliferation of Exploratory classes.

Definition of an Exploratory Class

The primary purpose of an Exploratory class is not that of extensive language acquisition. Exploratory classes are designed to provide an introduction to the study of a language and the related cultures. Minimal amounts of time are devoted to acquiring the language. Some commonly accepted goals of Exploratory classes are to:

- create an awareness of language as a vehicle for communication

- introduce the functional purpose of language study

- present the sound systems of another language

- instill an appreciation of other peoples and cultures

- provide motivation to continue learning another language

The typical Exploratory class is taught in grades 6–8 and lasts 4–12 weeks. Classes of longer duration provide students with the opportunity to go beyond the stages of simple exploration and begin rudimentary steps toward language acquisition.

When comparing several approaches to language study, it is essential to understand that exploration is one possible goal. Such exploration can create interest and encourage students to pursue a skills-based program where the goal is language acquisition and proficiency. These two goals, exploration and proficiency, are not incompatible, just different.

There is no specific grade level at which an Exploratory program should occur. However, the earlier Exploratory programs are offered, the earlier the opportunity to use them as the first step toward a sequence of language study. Learning a language is a skill-acquiring and skill-clarifying process. It takes time! Exploratory programs should immediately precede, and serve as a transition into, the regular sequential language program.

The placement of an Exploratory class at the beginning of middle school opens the door to language learning early. Early exploration leads to early opportunity to begin a skills-based program, thus making longer language sequences possible. It extends the process of language acquisition and gives students the opportunity to take advanced classes in high school.

Due to the introductory nature of the classes, not all Exploratory teachers are language specialists. While having a teacher certified in the language is optimal, the primary and most important qualifications are a positive attitude toward language learning and the ability to encourage students to pursue further study.

Characteristics of the Middle-School Learner

Young adolescents undergo tremendous physical and mental changes. They grow faster than at any time except for the first year of life. They are physically uncomfortable after sitting 20–25 minutes. Middle level students' physical "growing pains" are real! With these factors in mind, Exploratory class teachers need to involve students in activities such as total physical response (TPR), role-plays, skits, projects, and games.

This is a time when adolescents undertake the important tasks of forming personal identity, acquiring social skills, establishing personal autonomy, and developing discipline. Middle-school learners are usually more open-minded and willing to explore. Such willingness works to an Exploratory teacher's advantage in encouraging students to explore different languages and cultures.

Young adolescents are largely concrete, not abstract, learners. They have an average attention span of 11.5 minutes. Grammar, with its abstract concepts, is difficult for many adolescents. To help facilitate comprehension and communication, teachers should use concrete objects and examples that relate to students' daily lives.

Additional practice should create opportunities for students to work in teams and utilize visuals, props, and realia. Students like to cut, paste, color, and draw. Fortunately, these so-called "fun" activities actually promote language acquisition and offer the change of pace so essential to students whose attention spans are short and who have a strong need to be physically active.

Adolescents are primarily motivated by short-term goals. Career options, college opportunities, and the intrinsic value of learning another language are not likely to be meaningful to them. Good Exploratory materials need to help students see the relevance of a second language to their own lives. It is important to give them meaningful opportunities to see the language used in real-life situations in order to keep the language contextualized and the lessons task-focused.

Middle-level students are open and ready to learn, but they need activity and variety. Successful Exploratory class teachers move quickly from one activity to the next, remain flexible, and let the learners' natural curiosity lead them. High-interest themes and a "hands on" approach to introduce cultural information address the unique needs and interests of young adolescents. Interweaving discussions of culture with games in the target language gives students variety. A diversity of activities appeals to shorter attention spans and different learning styles. A slower pace accommodates the developmental level of middle school students.

Assessment

Whether or not grading is a part of your Exploratory classroom, assessment is still an important component. It gives credibility to the efforts you are asking of your students and can provide students and teachers a chance for self-evaluation. Assessment provides the opportunity for both teacher and student to evaluate accumulated knowledge and the achievement of lesson objectives.

For most students, a middle-school Exploratory class will be their first experience with another language. It will shape their attitudes and help them decide whether to pursue language study. For some students, it will be their only experience with another language. It is crucial that the teacher make the language-learning experience positive, informative, and motivational. Successful Exploratory language programs can provide strong support for sequential language programs by building student interest, and by increasing community awareness and appreciation for second-language learning.

The Holt Spanish Exploratory Guide

Provides motivation to learn another language by:

- ◆ Teaching multi-sensory language learning techniques.
- ◆ Modeling the use of language to communicate everyday topics, such as family, school, and sports.
- ◆ Explaining the sound systems of another language and providing many opportunities for students to hear native speakers.

Instills an appreciation of other peoples and cultures by:

- ◆ Including culture notes and activities in each lesson.
- ◆ Providing suggestions for projects on cultural topics.
- ◆ Offering cultural information through a video tour of the Spanish-speaking world.

Meets the special needs of middle school students by:

- ◆ Providing opportunities for role-plays, projects, learning games, and TPR (Total Physical Response).
- ◆ Giving suggestions for students to work in pairs, small groups, and teams.
- ◆ Providing students opportunities to cut, paste, color, and draw.
- ◆ Offering a diversity of activities for shorter attention spans and kinesthetic, tactile, and visual learning styles.
- ◆ Providing a measured pace appropriate for middle school students' developmental level.
- ◆ Emphasizing fun and opportunities for success with another language.

In addition to the Holt Spanish resources below, you will also need some readily available supplies for projects and other suggested in-class activities. See the following materials list or the Resource and Materials boxes at the beginning of each lesson for specific materials required in that lesson.

Holt Spanish Resources

- ◆ **Adelante** and **En camino**
  Annotated Teacher's Editions OR
  ¡Ven conmigo! Spanish 1 *Annotated Teacher's Edition*

 ◆ *DVD Tutor*

 ◆ *Interactive CD-ROM Tutor*

 ◆ *Teaching Transparencies*

 ◆ *Video Program*

◆ *Video Guide*

 ◆ *Audio Compact Discs*

◆ *Activities for Communication*

Additional Materials
Students and Teachers Will Need:

UNIT 1

Lesson 1
- Wall map of the world
- Copies of *Map Transparency 2*
- Cardboard, scissors, tape or glue

Lesson 2
- Wall map of Europe and Latin America
- List of words with ñ and rr
- Travel magazines

Lesson 3
- Pens, pencils, or other objects
- Index cards
- Magazines

Lesson 4
- Magazines
- Colored construction paper, scissors
- Tape or glue
- Colored markers, pencils, or crayons

Review and Assessment
- School supplies
- Encyclopedias or Internet resources
- Drawing paper
- Color flashcards

UNIT 2

Lesson 1
- Communicative Activity 1-1A / 1-1B
- Drawing paper
- Vocabulary cards with greetings

Lesson 2
- Transparency marker
- Pictures of people from magazines
- Flashcards with numbers
- Index cards, scissors, tape or glue

Lesson 3
- Copies of Teaching Transparency 1-B
- Index cards
- Two sets of vocabulary cards
- Scissors, tape or glue

Lesson 4
- Copies of Teaching Transparency 1-C
- Index cards, tape or glue, scissors
- Copies of Chapter 1 Video Activity Master 2
- Poster board, magazines

Review and Assessment
- Vocabulary flashcards
- Drawing paper

UNIT 3

Lesson 1
- Index cards
- Advertisements with pictures of school supplies
- Scissors, tape or glue

Lesson 2
- Flash cards 1–60
- Paper plate clock
- Project: paper plates, markers, construction paper, scissors, and brads

Lesson 3
- Calendar in Spanish
- Drawing paper

Lesson 4
- Magazines
- Poster board
- Scissors

Review and Assessment
- Paper-plate clocks
- School supplies
- Drawing paper

UNIT 4

Lesson 1
- Unit 2 sport vocabulary cards
- Magazine pictures of sports
- Drawing paper and markers

Lesson 2
- Transparency marker
- Magazine pictures or drawings of vocabulary items
- Clay or Play-doh®
- Tape or glue

Lesson 3
- Index cards
- Magazines, scissors
- Tape or glue
- Shoebox for each student
- Construction paper

Lesson 4
- Index cards
- Markers
- Drawing paper

Review and Assessment
- Vocabulary flashcards
- Magazines
- Drawing paper or poster board

UNIT 5

Lesson 1
- Index cards
- Magazines
- Tape or glue, scissors
- Transparency marker

Lesson 2
- Transparency marker
- Calendars
- Flashcards for months of the year

Lesson 3
- Construction paper
- Markers or colored pencils
- Magazines, scissors, tape or glue

Lesson 4
- Index cards
- Magazines
- Tape or glue
- Tissue paper, pencils, scissors
- Poster board, markers

Review and Assessment
- Vocabulary flashcards
- Drawing paper or butcher paper

UNIT 6

Lesson 1
- Index cards, glue, scissors
- Magazines, poster board, markers
- Empty food containers

Lesson 2
- Transparency marker
- Colored construction paper, scissors, glue
- Colored markers

Lesson 3
- Photos of food from magazines
- Construction paper, scissors, glue sticks, and pens, colored pencils or markers
- Drawing paper or poster board

Lesson 4
- Disposable plates, cups, forks, knives, and spoons
- Magazines that picture restaurants and dishes
- Food items made from construction paper from Lessons 2 and 3

Review and Assessment
- Unit 6 vocabulary flashcards
- Drawing paper

Additional Materials *continued*

UNIT 7

Lesson 1
- Index cards
- Travel magazines, scissors
- Drawing paper, pens, tape, or glue
- Name tags

Lesson 2
- Transparency marker
- Paper signs labeled with street names, tape
- City vocabulary cards from Unit 7, Lesson 1
- City maps from Unit 7, Lesson 1 Project

Lesson 3
- Index cards
- City maps from Lesson 1 and 2
- Rulers, scissors, markers or colored pencils

Lesson 4
- Nature magazines with photos of animals
- Index cards, scissors, tape or glue
- Large sheets of paper
- Markers, colored pencils, or paint

Review and Assessment
- Vocabulary flashcards for city and animals
- Drawing paper
- Markers or colored pencils
- Copy of Activity Master 7.2

UNIT 8

Lesson 1
- Copies of *Teaching Transparency 6-1*
- Drawing paper
- Magazines or newspapers
- Pictures of people
- Tape or glue, scissors

Lesson 2
- Paper and pens
- Foam ball

Lesson 3
- Index cards, scissors, tape or glue
- Magazines
- Drawing paper, markers or colored pencils

Lesson 4
- Magazine pictures of animals
- Index cards with animal pictures
- Blank transparency and transparency marker
- Poster paper, scissors, tape or glue

Review and Assessment
- Copies of *Teaching Transparency 6-1*
- Project: drawing paper, construction paper, markers, glue or tape, magazines or photos

UNIT 9

Lesson 1
- Clothing items from vocabulary list
- Paper, scissors
- Colored pens or paints
- Clothing catalogs, magazines, newspapers

Lesson 2
- Index cards
- Clothing items from the vocabulary list

Lesson 3
- Paper, markers or colored pencils
- Magazines, scissors, tape or glue

Lesson 4
- Index cards, magazines, scissors
- Thermometer, facial tissue, cough syrup, can of chicken soup
- Poster board, tape or glue

Review and Assessment
- Vocabulary flashcards
- Drawing paper, pencils or pens

UNIT 1 · ¡Bienvenidos!   Lesson 1   Geography and Culture

¡Ven conmigo! and Adelante Resources
- Map Transparency 2
- Video Program and Video Guide, Preliminary Chapter
- Interactive CD-ROM Tutor, Disc 1
- Adelante Annotated Teacher's Edition

Materials you will need
- Wall map of the world
- Copies of Map Transparency 2
- Cardboard, scissors, tape or glue

Language and Culture Objectives
Students will
- learn about where Spanish is spoken
- learn the names of Spanish-speaking countries

Motivate
- Ask students which states have Spanish names. (Colorado, Florida, Montana, Nevada) What are some cities with Spanish names? (San Francisco, San Antonio, Boca Raton) What comes to mind when they think of the Spanish-speaking world?

Teach
1. **Culture** To present information about where Spanish is spoken, play the Preliminary Chapter video and use page 1 of the corresponding guide. Pause the video and have students write the names of the three countries they are welcomed to at the beginning of the video. (Costa Rica, Venezuela, Argentina) Have students write the number of Spanish-speaking people in the world (over 340 million), and in the United States (over 25 million), as mentioned in the video. Explain that Spanish originated in Spain. The Spanish later colonized the Caribbean and the Americas and brought their language with them.

2. **Visual Learners** Show students Map Transparency 2 of the world with overlays to point out Spanish-speaking countries. See the Unit 1 Vocabulary list on page 9 for a list of countries. Ask students to name parts of the United States where many Spanish speakers live. (California, Arizona, New Mexico, Texas, Florida, New York)

3. **Listening** Hand out copies of the labeled blackline master of Map 2, **Europa y las**

Américas. Read a list of true and false statements about the location of certain cities and countries in English. Have students use the map to check your statements and indicate **cierto** or **falso** (true or false).

4. **Speaking** Have students work in pairs. One partner names the capital of a Spanish-speaking country and the other names the country.

5. **Writing** Have students complete Activity Master 1.1 to practice recognizing the location and names of Spanish-speaking countries.

Additional Practice
- **Visual Learners** Have students use the Interactive CD-ROM Tutor, Disc 1, Chapters 1 and 2, Spain Location Opener, to learn about Spain. Present the geography clues in **Enlaces** Activity 3 on page 51 in **Adelante**. Have students work in pairs to find where all four Spanish-speaking students live.

- **Project** Have students color an unlabeled copy of Map Transparency 2 world map, marking all the Spanish-speaking countries in one color. Have them label the Spanish-speaking countries and the major cities.

Close
- **Game** Have students mount unlabeled maps of the Spanish-speaking world on cardboard and cut out the countries along their borders. Divide students into two teams and place the puzzle pieces in a bag. Have a player from the first team draw a piece from the bag and identify the country within 15 seconds. If the player answers correctly, award the team a point. If the player's answer is incorrect, award the point to the other team. Continue until all puzzle pieces have been identified.

Activity Master 1.1   Geography and Culture

1 Label the Spanish-speaking countries of Central America and the Caribbean. Write the number of the country on the country itself.

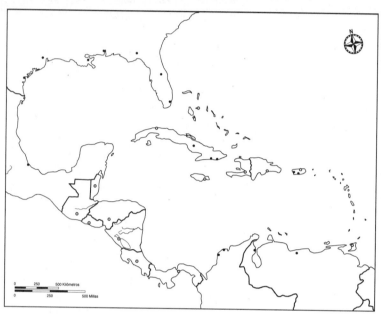

1. República Dominicana

2. Honduras

3. Puerto Rico

4. El Salvador

5. Cuba

6. Nicaragua

7. Guatemala

8. Costa Rica

9. Panamá

2 Find 14 Spanish-speaking countries hidden in the puzzle below. Words appear vertically and horizontally.

Argentina
Chile
Bolivia
España
República Dominicana
México
Guinea Ecuatorial
Colombia
Ecuador   Perú
Uruguay
Paraguay
Venezuela
Puerto Rico

```
I L B A M U E S E A G A C Y P É F I N
G U I N E A E C U A T O R I A L B C L
U G A N X I H Ñ S E I U T T Ú C O S I
E R C H I L E U B A B R F O S R L Ñ A
T I N U C G U A T E C U A D O R I N R
P L É E U P U E R T O R I C O A V A G
U V Y C D A O I Ñ L L P A E X L I R P
R E P Ú B L I C A D O M I N I C A N A
U N E I E O G R C B M Z P A H O S I R
G E R D P S Q U H O B D U G A Y M C A
U Z Ú A T Ñ E R I L I P E V S T É A G
A U T R D S H I L P A R R T G A X R U
Y E R A S E S P A Ñ A R G E N T I N A
B L U R U G U X A N T Y O L C I C G Y
Ñ A R G E Ñ T I N I S A R E I C O U B
Y R U E L O Z S I M U X I A W A R A L
```

UNIT 1 · ¡Bienvenidos! Lesson 2 The Alphabet

¡Ven conmigo! and Adelante Resources

- *Map Transparency 2*
- *Audio Program,* Audio CD 1
- *Video Program,* Preliminary Chapter
- *Adelante* OR *¡Ven conmigo! Annotated Teacher's Edition*

Materials you will need

- Wall map of Europe and Latin America
- List of words with **ñ** and **rr**
- Travel magazines

Language and Culture Objectives

Students will

- learn the Spanish alphabet
- learn about culture of Spanish-speaking countries
- learn how to ask someone's name and tell theirs

Motivate

- Play the Preliminary Chapter video segment in which two girls recite the alphabet. Ask which letter was missing. (**n**)

Teach

1. *Auditory Learners* Write the letters of the Spanish alphabet on the board. Then have students listen to the alphabet on Audio CD 1, Track 3. See the *Adelante Annotated Teacher's Edition* for the script.

2. *Culture* Have students copy the letters of the Spanish alphabet onto a piece of paper. Ask them to circle the different letters (**ch, ll, ñ, rr**). Recite the letters of the alphabet aloud, or play the audio again and have students repeat after you.

3. *Visual Learners* Model spelling the names of some Spanish-speaking countries as students repeat them and look at a wall map or *Map Transparency 2* of **Europa y las Américas.** Then have students spell the names of Central American countries in Spanish with a partner. Next they take turns spelling the names of South American countries as the partner tries to guess them in as few letters as possible.

4. *Speaking* Teach students how to ask someone's name, **¿Cómo te llamas?** and how to answer **Me llamo...** Have students introduce themselves to a classmate.

5. *Challenge* Spell students' first or last names in Spanish and ask them to raise their hands when they recognize theirs. Have pairs of students spell their first and last names to each other using the Spanish alphabet.

6. *Writing* Have students complete Activity Master 1.2 to practice the Spanish alphabet. Read the script for Activity 1. The listening script with answers in parentheses follows: 1. te-e-equis-a-ese (Texas); 2. ce-u-be-a (Cuba); 3. pe-e-ere-u (Perú); 4. eme-i-a-eme-i (Miami); 5. e-ese-pe-a-eñe-a (España)

Additional Practice

- *Listening* Have students recite the rhyme **A e i o u, Arbolito de Perú** to practice vowel sounds in Spanish. Play Audio CD 1 Track 2 *(Adelante)* or Audio CD 1 Track 4 *(¡Ven conmigo!)* to have students listen to Spanish speakers spell their names. See *Adelante* or *¡Ven conmigo! Annotated Teacher's Edition,* page T69 or T75, for the script. Have students write each name as they hear it spelled.

- *Project* Have students look in magazines for pictures of people, places, or things with names that include **ñ** and **rr**. For example, **ñ: España, piñata, señor, señorita** *(Spain, piñata, Mr., Miss)* and **rr: burro, carro** *(donkey, car).*

Close

- *Game* Teach students the question **¿Es una...?** Write random letters on the board, point to one, and ask **¿Es una ere?,** for example. Students respond with a thumbs up or thumbs down. Then dictate words letter by letter. Try including names of famous people, local sports stars, and the names of cities in Spanish-speaking countries. Have students write the words on the board or on paper.

UNIT 1

Activity Master 1.2   The Alphabet

1 Listen as you hear five words being spelled out in Spanish. Write the letters you hear.

1. ____ ____ ____ ____ ____   4. ____ ____ ____ ____ ____

2. ____ ____ ____ ____   5. ____ ____ ____ ____ ____ ____

3. ____ ____ ____ ____

2 Use the words in the box to write the cognates in the spaces provided. Cognates are words that both came from the same parent language. They are similar to each other in spelling and meaning, but are usually pronounced differently.

| rosa | helicóptero | león | serpiente | arte | trompeta | cebra |

1. _____

2. _____

3. _____

4. _____

5. _____

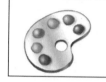

6. _____

7. _____

3 Work with a partner. Take turns spelling the answers to the following questions in Spanish. Use the blank to write the information your partner says and say the word aloud to confirm that you both got it right.

Ask your partner: How do you spell . . .

1. your last name? _____

2. the name of your favorite actor? _____

3. the name of your favorite movie? _____

4. the name of your favorite music group? _____

5. the name of a city you would like to visit? _____

UNIT 1 · ¡Bienvenidos!   Lesson 3   Numbers 0–20

U N I T 1

¡Ven conmigo! and Adelante Resources	Materials you will need
• *Teaching Transparency 1-A* • *Adelante* OR *¡Ven conmigo! Annotated Teacher's Edition* • *Video Program,* Preliminary Chapter • *Audio Compact Discs,* CD 1 • *Interactive CD-ROM Tutor,* Disc 1	• Pens, pencils, or other objects • Index cards • Magazines

Language and Culture Objectives

Students will
• learn to count to 20 in Spanish
• learn about the culture of Spanish-speaking countries

Motivate

• Ask students when they use numbers each day. (to tell time, to buy things, to do math problems) Play the sections of the Preliminary Chapter video about the daily use of numbers.

Teach

1. **Visual Learners** Display *Teaching Transparency 1-A* and point to each number as you pronounce it for the class and have students repeat. Have students count on their fingers starting with the thumb as shown on page 14 of *Adelante* or page 9 of *¡Ven conmigo!*

2. **Kinesthetic Learners** Have students repeat after you as you count. Have them count up to ten both aloud and on their fingers. Hold up several pencils, pens, or other objects and ask students **¿Cuántos son?** Have students answer by saying the number in Spanish and holding up the correct number of fingers.

3. **Language Learning** Have students use index cards to make flashcards of the numbers 0–20. They write the numerals on one side and the words in Spanish on the other.

4. **Listening** Have students use their number flashcards to hold up the correct numbers as you say them in Spanish.

5. *Game* Divide the class into two or three groups and have each sit in a circle. Give each student a number from one to ten. Student one begins by calling out his or her own number, **uno**, and another person's

number, for example, **siete**. Seven then calls out **siete** and another person's number, **dos**, for example. If someone makes an error in calling someone's number and says the wrong word, they become the last number in the circle, and everyone with a larger number moves up one place. The object is to get to the number one place.

6. *Writing* Have students complete Activity Master 1.1 to practice writing numbers in Spanish.

Additional Practice

• *Listening* Play the listening activity **Números de teléfono** on *Adelante* Audio CD 1 Track 4 or *¡Ven conmigo!* Activity 13, Audio CD 1 Track 8. Play the Preliminary Chapter video for an additional example of counting up to 11.

• *Project* Have students write and illustrate a list of objects that correspond to the numbers 1–10. They may draw the items or clip pictures from magazines and label the number they represent in Spanish.

• *Visual Learners* Have students use *Interactive CD-ROM Tutor,* Chapter 1, Activity 3, to practice the numbers 0–10.

• *Group Work* Teach students the words **más** and **son** (*plus* and *equals*) so they can quiz each other with simple addition problems.

Close

• *Game* **Adivina Adivinador** Have a student think of a number between 1 and 20. Have students try to guess the number. When they guess, the person with the secret number gives them hints by saying **más** or **menos** (*more/less*). The person who guesses the number correctly chooses the next one.

Activity Master 1.3   Numbers 0–20

UNIT 1

1 Color in the squares according to the number in each. Use the color key below the chart. What country's name do you find?

1	1	1	1	1	1	1	3	3	3	3	3	3	3	4	4	4	4	4	4	4
1	1	1	1	1	1	1	3	3	3	3	3	3	3	4	4	4	4	4	4	4
1	1	1	1	1	1	1	3	3	3	3	3	3	3	4	4	4	4	4	4	4
1	1	1	1	1	1	1	3	3	3	3	3	3	3	4	4	4	4	4	4	4
1	1	1	1	1	1	1	3	3	3	3	3	3	3	4	4	4	4	4	4	4
2	1	2	1	2	2	2	3	2	3	2	3	2	3	2	2	2	4	2	2	2
2	2	2	1	2	1	1	3	2	3	2	3	2	3	2	4	4	4	2	4	2
2	1	2	1	2	2	2	3	3	2	3	3	2	3	2	4	4	4	2	4	2
2	1	2	1	2	1	1	3	3	2	3	3	2	3	2	4	4	4	2	4	2
2	1	2	1	2	1	1	3	2	3	2	3	2	3	2	4	4	4	2	4	2
2	1	2	1	2	2	2	3	2	3	2	3	2	3	2	2	2	4	2	2	2
1	1	1	1	1	1	1	3	3	3	3	3	3	3	4	4	4	4	4	4	4
1	1	1	1	1	1	1	3	3	3	3	3	3	3	4	4	4	4	4	4	4
1	1	1	1	1	1	1	3	3	3	3	3	3	3	4	4	4	4	4	4	4
1	1	1	1	1	1	1	3	3	3	3	3	3	3	4	4	4	4	4	4	4
1	1	1	1	1	1	1	3	3	3	3	3	3	3	4	4	4	4	4	4	4

uno = verde *(green)*   **dos = negro** *(black)*   **tres = blanco** *(white)*   **cuatro = rojo** *(red)*

2 Write the correct numeral for the number in Spanish.

uno   _____   veinte   _____   nueve   _____

seis   _____   quince   _____   diecisiete _____

3 What numbers come to mind for each of the following items? Write the numbers in Spanish.

1. wheels on a bicycle _____   6. tentacles on an octopus _____
2. sides in a triangle _____   7. days in a week _____
3. legs on a chair _____   8. eggs in a dozen _____
4. fingers on one hand _____   9. toes on both feet _____
5. stripes on the
   United States' flag _____   10. cats on the moon _____

4 Write the word in Spanish for the answers to these math problems.

1. 3 + 3 =   _____   6. 23 - 7 = _____
2. 5 + 10 =   _____   7. 8 - 5 =   _____
3. 7 + 13 =   _____   8. 19 - 18 = _____
4. 16 + 2 =   _____   9. 20 - 6 = _____
5. 4 + 3 + 2 = _____   10. 15 - 4 = _____

UNIT 1 · ¡Bienvenidos!   Lesson 4   Colors

¡Ven conmigo! and Adelante Resources
- *Teaching Transparency 1-1*
- *Video Program,* Preliminary Chapter
- *Adelante Annotated Teacher's Edition*

Materials you will need
- Magazines
- Colored construction paper, scissors
- Tape or glue
- Colored markers, pencils, or crayons

Language and Culture Objectives

Students will
- learn the names of colors in Spanish
- learn about the culture of Spanish-speaking countries

Motivate
- Ask students to stand if they are wearing blue, black, and so on. What color is worn by the most people in class today?

Teach
1. *Visual Learners* Display a color wheel, objects of different colors, or colored construction paper to present the colors. Have students repeat the names of the colors after you. Show *Teaching Transparency 1-1.* Point to people's articles of clothing and say **Es rojo,** for example. Have students repeat after you, **Es rojo.**

2. *Kinesthetic Learners* Call out a color in Spanish and have students wearing that color stand and point to the article of clothing that is that color.

3. *Auditory Learners* Call out a color and have students raise their hands and say a fruit, vegetable, or animal that is that color.

4. *Speaking* Ask students true and false questions (**cierto o falso**) ¿**Es rojo?** for the color of objects in the room. Ask students what their favorite color is. (¿**Cuál es tu color preferido?**)

5. *Language Learning* Have students cut colored construction paper into squares and distribute them so each student has one square of each color. Have students arrange the papers left to right or top to bottom on their desks in the order you name the colors. You may have students write the Spanish word for the color on their pieces of construction paper at the end to use them as flash cards.

6. *Writing* Have students use Activity Master 1.4 to practice the words for colors in Spanish.

Additional Practice
- *Listening* Say a color in Spanish and hold up a color flashcard. If the color name does not match the color card, students hold up the correct color square. If the color name and the color square match, students hold up their matching color card and repeat the name of the color aloud.

- *Visual Learners* Have students watch the **Panorama cultural** portion of the Preliminary Chapter Video or Videodisc. Stop right after each student introduces him or herself and have students name the colors in the country flags in Spanish.

- *Project* Have students cut out pictures from magazines to make color collages, labeling the color in Spanish.

Close
- *Game* Have students color the squares of a **PONGA** *(Bingo®)* game. Call out names of colors and have students cover the appropriate squares with pieces of paper. For more detailed instructions on how to play **PONGA,** see page 19I of *Adelante Annotated Teacher's Edition.*

Nombre _____ Clase _____ Fecha _____

UNIT 1

1 Color the flag of Puerto Rico. Use the colors written on the flag.

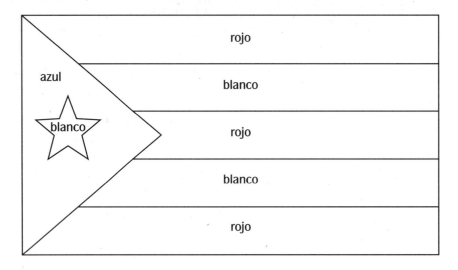

rojo

azul

blanco

blanco

rojo

blanco

rojo

2 What colors come to mind for the following things?

1. a lemon _____

2. the sky on a clear day _____

3. autumn leaves (list three) _____,

_____ y _____

4. grass _____

5. grape bubble gum _____

6. a fire engine _____

7. a blizzard _____

8. words on this page _____

3 Color the design below. This design is similar to tiles used in the Alhambra in Granada, Spain. The Alhambra is a castle built beginning in the ninth century during the Moorish occupation of Spain. Use the colors written on the tiles.

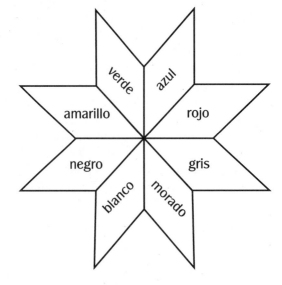

verde

azul

amarillo

rojo

negro

gris

blanco

morado

UNIT 1 · ¡Bienvenidos! *Welcome!*   **Vocabulary**

LESSON 1 · Geography and Culture

Argentina	Honduras
Bolivia	México
Chile	Nicaragua
Colombia	Panamá
Costa Rica	Paraguay
Cuba	Perú
Ecuador	Puerto Rico
El Salvador	República Dominicana
España *Spain*	*Dominican Republic*
Guatemala	Uruguay
Guinea Ecuatorial *Ecuatorial Guinea*	Venezuela

LESSON 2 · The Alphabet

a	a	i	i	p	pe	x	equis
b	be	j	jota	q	cu	y	i griega
c	ce	k	ka	r	ere	z	zeta
ch	che	l	ele	rr	erre	**¿Cómo te llamas?**	
d	de	ll	elle	s	ese	*What is your*	
e	e	m	eme	t	te	*name?*	
f	efe	n	ene	u	u	**Me llamo...**	
g	ge	ñ	eñe	v	ve	*My name is . . .*	
h	hache	o	o	w	doble ve		

LESSON 3 · Numbers 0–20

cero *zero*	**ocho** *eight*	**dieciséis** *sixteen*
uno *one*	**nueve** *nine*	**diecisiete** *seventeen*
dos *two*	**diez** *ten*	**dieciocho** *eighteen*
tres *three*	**once** *eleven*	**diecinueve** *nineteen*
cuatro *four*	**doce** *twelve*	**veinte** *twenty*
cinco *five*	**trece** *thirteen*	**más** *more, plus*
seis *six*	**catorce** *fourteen*	**menos** *less, minus*
siete *seven*	**quince** *fifteen*	**son** *equals* (or *are*)

LESSON 4 · Colors

amarillo *yellow*	**morado** *purple*
anaranjado *orange*	**negro** *black*
azul *blue*	**rojo** *red*
blanco *white*	**rosado** *pink*
gris *gray*	**verde** *green*
marrón *brown*	

UNIT 1 · ¡Bienvenidos!   **Review and Assessment**

UNIT 1

¡Ven conmigo! and *Adelante* Resources
- *Interactive CD-ROM Tutor,* Disc 1

Materials you will need
- School supplies
- Encyclopedias or Internet resources
- Drawing paper
- Color flashcards

Language and Culture Assessment Objectives

Students will

- show their knowledge of the names of Spanish-speaking countries, the alphabet, numbers and color vocabulary in Spanish

- show their knowledge of culture related to the Spanish-speaking world

- express their knowledge orally and in the form of an in-class project

Review

1. Have students count to 20 as a class. They clap as they say the number in Spanish. Place several different kinds of school supplies on a table and have students count them aloud.

2. Call out colors and have students hold up their correct color flashcard.

3. Have students say the alphabet. Have one student start with **a,** the next continue with **be,** and so on around the classroom.

4. Have students ask and tell each other the color of their socks or shoes.

5. Have students name as many Spanish-speaking countries as they can. For a challenge, ask if they can spell them aloud in Spanish.

Assessment Options

Written
- Have students complete ¡**Ya lo sé!**, Unit 1. You will find the script for the listening activity on page 113 of this guide.

- *Project* Have students work on a project about a Spanish-speaking country of their choice. The project should include a colored drawing of the flag with the colors labeled in Spanish, and a map of the country with the names of the major cities labeled.

Oral

1. Place five different color squares on the student's desk for the student to name.

2. Hold up a number of fingers and ask the student ¿**Cuántos son?**

3. Ask the student to spell his or her first name in Spanish.

4. Ask the student a true or false question about an article of clothing he or she is wearing. For example, gesture to his or her shoe and ask ¿**Es azul?** The student responds **cierto** or **falso.**

5. Ask the student to name two countries where Spanish is spoken.

6. Ask the student to spell **Nicaragua** or another Spanish-speaking country in Spanish. Allow students to look at the word as they spell it.

CD-ROM
- Use *Interactive CD-ROM Tutor* Disc 1, Chapter 1, Activity 3, Concentration®, to assess students on number vocabulary 1–10.

UNIT 1 · ¡Bienvenidos!   **¡Ya lo sé!**   **Total Points: 40**

UNIT 1

A. The Alphabet

Listen as your teacher spells the names of five countries aloud. Write them in the spaces below. (10 points)

1. _____

2. _____

3. _____

4. _____

5. _____

SCORE _____

B. Colors

What colors come to mind when you think of the following items? Write the colors in Spanish. (10 points)

 _____ y

1. _____

2. _____

3. _____

4. _____

5. _____

SCORE _____

UNIT 1 · ¡Bienvenidos!   ¡Ya lo sé!   *continued*

UNIT 1

C. Numbers

In the first column, write the numeral for each Spanish word. In the second column, write
the Spanish word for each numeral. (16 points)

1. _____ diez   5. _____ 18

2. _____ siete   6. _____ 14

3. _____ trece   7. _____ 2

4. _____ seis   8. _____ 9

SCORE [   ]

D. El español

Write the names of four Spanish-speaking countries on the map of South America below.
Use the country names in the word box to label four of the nine countries. (4 points)

Colombia

Paraguay

Chile

Perú

Argentina

Uruguay

Ecuador

Venezuela

Bolivia

SCORE [   ]

TOTAL SCORE [/40]

UNIT 2 · Getting Acquainted   Lesson 1   Greetings

¡Ven conmigo! and Adelante Resources
- *Teaching Transparency 1-1*
- *Audio Compact Discs*, CD 1
- *Activities for Communication*, Chapter 1
- *Interactive CD-ROM Tutor*, Disc 1

Materials you will need
- Copies of Communicative Activity 1-1A and 1-1B
- Drawing paper
- Vocabulary cards with greetings

Language and Culture Objectives
Students will
- learn about formal and informal greetings
- learn phrases to greet people

Motivate
- Ask students what they say to greet their classmates. What do they say to greet their teachers? Are there differences? If so, why?

Teach
1. *Visual Learners*   Display *Teaching Transparency 1-1* to present greetings. Teach students **Buenas tardes** *(Good afternoon)* for the first picture and **Buenos días** *(Good morning)* for the second picture. Draw a rising sun, a setting sun, and the moon and some stars on the board. Have students say the appropriate greetings for each time of day. Teach students how to say *goodbye* (**Adiós**).

2. *Culture*   Lead a discussion about formal and informal greetings in Spanish-speaking countries. Tell students that, in general, younger people use informal greetings with their friends and use formal greetings to show respect with teachers, parents, and strangers. Teach students to ask how people are in Spanish. Explain that **¿Cómo estás?** is used for friends and **¿Cómo está usted?** for teachers, adults, and strangers. Have them repeat after you, then model an answer, **Estoy bien, gracias.** *(I'm fine, thanks.)*

3. *Kinesthetic Learners*   To introduce other expressions, draw a smiling face (**bien**), a neutral face (**regular**), and a frowning face (**mal, muy mal**) on the board and write the appropriate expressions under each face.

Say each expression and have students repeat them and make the appropriate face to show what it means.

4. *Listening*   List these six names on the board: 1. Alicia; 2. Santiago; 3. don Alonso; 4. Mariana; 5. doña Luisa; 6. David. Have students copy them. Then play Activity 5 on *Adelante* Chapter 1 Audio CD 1, Track 11. For *¡Ven conmigo!* materials play Activity 6 on Audio CD 1, Track 11. Have students listen and circle the names of the people who are arriving.

5. *Speaking*   Have student pairs practice greeting each other in Spanish. Have them role-play two friends greeting each other and then role-play a student and an older person greeting each other. Ask volunteers to perform their role-plays for the class.

6. *Writing*   Have students use Activity Master 2.1 to practice greetings in Spanish.

7. *Visual Learners*   Have students use the *Interactive CD-ROM Tutor,* Disc 1, Chapter 1, Activities 1 and 2 to practice greetings.

Additional Practice
- *Speaking*   Have students do Communicative Activity 1-1A and 1-1B in pairs.
- *Project*   Have students draw a comic strip in which two people meet, exchange greetings, ask the other how he or she is doing, and say goodbye in Spanish.

Close
- *Game*   **Charades** Have students work in pairs. Hand out one greeting vocabulary card to each pair of students. The pair should act out the greeting for the class and have the class guess which greeting it is.

UNIT 2

Activity Master 2.1   Greetings

1 Match each of the following short conversations with the drawings.

_____ 1.

— Hasta luego,
    Rita y Gregorio.

— ¡Adiós!

_____ 2.

— Buenas tardes,
    señora Sánchez.

— Hola, Marisa.

_____ 3.

— Hola, señorita
    Martínez.

— Buenas noches, Tomás.

2 A number of people have just been asked **¿Cómo estás?** Match each response with the drawing that best shows how the person is doing.

_____ 1. ¡Estoy bien!

_____ 2. Estoy regular.

_____ 3. ¡Bien, gracias!

_____ 4. Estoy muy mal.

_____ 5. Estoy muy bien.

3 Match the phrases below to one of the drawings of Teresa, according to whether she is talking *about herself* or asking about *you.* Write **a** or **b** in the blanks.

_____ 1. Me llamo Teresa.

_____ 2. ¿Cómo te llamas?

_____ 3. Estoy bien.

_____ 4. Estoy regular.

_____ 5. ¿Cómo estás?

UNIT 2

UNIT 2 · Getting Acquainted — Lesson 2 — Age

¡Ven conmigo! and Adelante Resources
- *Teaching Transparency 1-A*
- *Interactive CD-ROM Tutor,* Disc 1

Materials you will need
- Transparency marker
- Pictures of people from magazines
- Flashcards with numbers
- Index cards, scissors, tape or glue

Language and Culture Objectives
Students will
- learn about coming-of-age parties
- learn phrases to talk about age

Motivate
- Ask students what special events we have in our society when people reach a certain age. (first communion, bar or bat mitzvah, first time to babysit, getting a driver's license.)

Teach
1. *Culture* Many Spanish-speaking girls celebrate a special coming-of-age celebration when they turn 15. It's called **una fiesta de quinceañera.** It can range from a small, informal gathering to a celebration as elaborate as a wedding. Usually the **padrino** *(godfather)* or **madrina** *(godmother)* presents the **quinceañera** with a special gift.

2. *Visual Learners* Show students *Teaching Transparency 1-A* of the numbers 21–30. Write the numbers and words in Spanish for forty, fifty, and sixty on the transparency as well. Have students make flashcards for the numbers 21–30, 40, 50 and 60 with the numeral on one side and the word in Spanish on the other. Tell students that for numbers between 30 and 99, three words are used: **treinta y uno** (31), **cuarenta y tres** (43), **cincuenta y seis** (56), **sesenta y ocho** (68).

3. *Game* Tell students that to ask someone their own age how old he or she is, they say **¿Cuántos años tienes?** Model a sample answer, for example, **Tengo 12 años.** Have students repeat the questions and answers after you. Then give a number flashcard to each student. Have students pretend that the number represents their age. Students arrange themselves in ascending order according to age without showing each other their numbers by asking **¿Cuántos años tienes?** and responding **Tengo ... años.** Next, model talking about someone else's age by asking one student another student's age, **¿Cuántos años tiene** (name)? **(Tiene ... años).**

4. *Listening* Post on the board five pictures clipped from magazines of people of easily distinguishable ages. Number them one to five. Have students number a sheet of paper from one to five. Then read sentences describing the five people. For example, **Don José tiene cincuenta y cinco años.** If **Don José** is #3, students would write 55 next to the item number. Check students' answers.

5. *Writing* Assign Activity Master 2.2 to have students practice numbers and talking about age.

6. *Visual Learners* Have students use the *Interactive CD-ROM Tutor,* Disc 1, Chapter 1, **Panorama cultural,** to listen to native speakers talk about their age.

Additional Practice
- *Project* Have students use magazines to create collages of pictures of people. Ask students to label their collages. The label for each picture should include a name and an age. For example, **La señora Pérez tiene cuarenta y cinco años.**

Close
- *Game* **Número secreto** Have students work in pairs. Each student writes five secret numbers between 1 and 60. Partners take turns guessing each other's numbers in Spanish. If a guess is wrong, the partner says **más** for a *higher* number or **menos** for a *lower* one. The other partner continues stating numbers until he or she guesses the number correctly.

UNIT 2

Activity Master 2.2   Age

1 Look at the illustrations below. First write the question you would use to ask your friend how old he or she is. Then match the letter of the person with the sentence that describes how old he or she is.

ⓐ   ⓑ   ⓒ   ⓓ

Question: ¿_____?

_____ **1.** Silvia tiene veinte años.   _____ **3.** Cristina tiene dos años.

_____ **2.** Leonardo tiene cuatro años.   _____ **4.** Rodolfo tiene catorce años.

2 Write out these math problems and solve the equation. Use the **modelo** as an example.

MODELO $2 + 8 =$ **Dos más ocho son diez.**

1. $4 + 15 =$ _____

2. $12 + 14 =$ _____

3. $11 + 13 =$ _____

4. $36 + 24 =$ _____

5. $45 + 7 =$ _____

3 Read the information given. Then write a sentence telling how old each person probably is.

MODELO   Pablo has a summer job. **Tiene quince años.**

1. Raquel just started kindergarten.

_____

2. Flavio just graduated from high school.

_____

3. Rosario just started sixth grade.

_____

4. Paco just started eighth grade.

_____

UNIT 2 · Getting Acquainted   Lesson 3   Sports and Classes

¡Ven conmigo! and *Adelante* Resources
- *Teaching Transparencies 1-B* and *1-3*
- *Adelante Annotated Teacher's Edition*

Materials you will need
- Copies of *Teaching Transparency 1-B*
- Index cards
- Two sets of vocabulary cards
- Scissors, tape or glue

Language and Culture Objectives
Students will
- learn cultural information about **fútbol**
- learn phrases to talk about likes and dislikes
- learn vocabulary for sports and school

Motivate
- Write *Sports* and *School* as column heads on the board. Ask students to name some things in English that they like and don't like in each category. Write their responses under the category heads.

Teach
1. *Culture* Explain that **fútbol** is the word for *soccer* in Spanish. In Spanish *football* is **fútbol norteamericano.** Tell students that soccer is the most popular sport in most Spanish-speaking countries and that football is not common.

2. *Visual Learners* Use *Teaching Transparency 1-B* or *Teaching Transparency 1-3* to present sports and school vocabulary. Say the vocabulary aloud and have students repeat the words. Model the phrases **Me gusta..., No me gusta...,** and **¿Te gusta...?** Have the class repeat them. Then ask students if they agree with statements you make, for example: **Me gusta el fútbol.**

3. *Language Learning* Hand out copies of *Teaching Transparency 1-B.* To create flashcards, students cut pictures from their copy and tape them to one side of an index card. They write the Spanish word on the other side. Students may also choose to draw pictures representing vocabulary words on the

index cards. Then have students work in pairs testing each other on the new vocabulary.

4. *Listening* Talk about sports you like and don't like. Have students use the flashcards they made in the previous activity. Ask them to hold up the correct card for each sport you like. If you don't like the sport, have students leave the card on their desks.

5. *Speaking* Hand out a sport vocabulary card to each student. Have students find their "twin," the student who has the same vocabulary word. Have them go around the room asking **¿Te gusta...?** to find their twin and answering their classmates' questions, **Sí, me gusta...** or **No, no me gusta...**

6. *Writing* Have students use Activity Master 2.3 to practice sports and school vocabulary and phrases for likes and dislikes.

Additional Practice
- *Culture* Present **Enlaces** on page 177 of *Adelante Annotated Teacher's Edition,* about Spanish-speaking countries' participation in the Olympics.

- *Project* Have students make a comic strip in which two people talk about their likes and dislikes. Ask students to use vocabulary from this lesson.

Close
- *Game* **Dibújalo** (Pictionary®) Divide the class into two teams. Have one student from each team come forward to draw on the board. Show a vocabulary word to both students. The students then draw pictures of the word and their teams try to guess the word in Spanish. The first team to guess the word wins a point.

UNIT 2

Nombre _____ Clase _____ Fecha _____

1 Write a sentence about a class you like and another sentence about a class you don't like. Then write a sentence about a sport you like and another sentence about a sport you don't like.

el fútbol
el tenis
la geografía
la clase de español
el voleibol
la tarea
el baloncesto
el béisbol
la clase de inglés

LAS CLASES

1. _____

2. _____

LOS DEPORTES

3. _____

4. _____

2 Samuel and Francisco want to play a sport together but there's only one sport they both like. Fill in the missing words in each boy's statements according to the sports equipment each boy has in the drawing. The answer may be one or two words.

Samuel

1.   **SAMUEL**   ¿_____ gusta el tenis?

    FRANCISCO   A mí no _____ el tenis.

2.   **SAMUEL**   ¿_____ gusta la natación?

    FRANCISCO   A mí _____ mucho la natación.

3.   **FRANCISCO**   A mí _____ el béisbol.

    SAMUEL   Pues a mí no me gusta _____.

4.   **SAMUEL**   ¿_____ el baloncesto?

    FRANCISCO   ¡Sí, me gusta muchísimo!

Francisco

UNIT 2 · Getting Acquainted   Lesson 4   Music and Food

¡Ven conmigo! and *Adelante/En camino* Resources

- *Teaching Transparency 1-C*
- *Audio Compact Discs,* CDs 1, 7, and 10
- *Interactive CD-ROM Tutor,* Disc 1
- *Adelante/En camino* Annotated Teacher's Edition

Materials you will need

- Copies of *Teaching Transparency 1-C*
- Index cards, tape or glue
- Copies of Chapter 1 Video Activity Master 2
- Scissors
- Poster board, magazines

Language and Culture Objectives

Students will

- learn cultural information about food
- learn vocabulary to talk about music and food

Motivate

- Ask students what kinds of music and food they like. Tell them they will learn how to talk about them in Spanish in this lesson.

Teach

1. *Culture*   Ask students what foods they think people eat in Spanish-speaking countries. List the suggestions on the board. Students may be the most familiar with Mexican food. Explain that different countries eat different kinds of foods according to what grows in their area. Tortillas, beans, and rice are common foods in Mexico and Central America. Pork is popular among Cubans and Puerto Ricans. Potatoes are a common food in Ecuador, Bolivia, and Peru. There are large cattle ranches in Argentina and Uruguay and people eat more beef there. For more cultural information about food, see *¡Ven conmigo!* or *En camino,* Chapter 8.

2. *Visual Learners*   Use *Teaching Transparency 1-C* to introduce vocabulary for music and food. Talk about the music and food you like. Have students repeat the phrases after you.

3. *Listening*   Play *Adelante* Activity 28 or *¡Ven conmigo!* Activity 29. *Adelante* Audio CD 1, Track 20 or *¡Ven conmigo!* Audio CD 1, Track 21. As students listen, have them write Elena's name next to the items she likes in the **Me gusta** column and dislikes in the **No me gusta** column. Have them do the same for Carlos. As a cumulative activity, ask students which item both cousins like.

4. *Language Learning*   Have students make flashcards for music and food vocabulary. Hand out copies of the blackline master of *Teaching Transparency 1-C* or have students draw pictures of the vocabulary on index cards. Ask students to write the word in Spanish on the other side. In pairs, students test each other on the new vocabulary.

5. *Writing*   Have students complete Activity Master 2.4 to reinforce music, food, sports and school vocabulary, and phrases about likes and dislikes.

6. *Visual Learners*   Have students use *Interactive CD-ROM Tutor,* Disc 1, Chapter 1, Activity 6, to practice sports, food, and music vocabulary.

Additional Practice

- *Culture*   Present **Enlaces** on page 176 of *Adelante, Annotated Teacher's Edition,* which is about different kinds of music in Spanish-speaking countries. Play songs such as **El cóndor pasa** and **Las mañanitas** from Audio CDs 7 and 10.

- *Project*   Have students make a poster illustrating three things they like and three things they don't like. Have them use only vocabulary from this unit. They can draw pictures or cut them out of magazines. Students should label their illustrations **Me gusta el/la...** or **No me gusta el/la....**

Close

- *Game*   Divide the class into two teams. Have students act out the vocabulary for sports, school, food, and music by playing charades.

Activity Master 2.4   **Music and Food**

1 Each of the seven groups of letters is a scrambled vocabulary word. Unscramble each one and write the letters in the blanks. Then arrange the circled letters to find the answer to the question **¿Qué te gusta?**

◯ __ __ __ __ ZAZPI

__ __ __ __ ◯ ARTFU

__ ◯ __ __ OÑSA

__ __ ◯ __ __ __ CIMÚSA

__ __ __ __ __ ◯ LOBSIBÉ

◯ __ __ __ __ __ __ __ NASAEALD

__ __ __ __ __ ◯ __ OBLOIVLE

voleibol   fruta
ensalada   años
pizza   música
béisbol

SOLUCIÓN: ME GUSTA EL __ __ __ __ __ __ __

2 Read the following lists of students' favorite things from specific categories. In each list, find the item that doesn't belong and circle it.

1. el chocolate	la música jazz	la música rock
2. la comida china	la natación	la pizza
3. el fútbol	el tenis	la comida italiana
4. la ensalada	la tarea	la comida mexicana
5. el español	la música clásica	la música pop

3 Write a sentence in Spanish for each drawing. Say whether you like or don't like what is shown.

MODELO   **No me gusta el béisbol.**

1.

**el fútbol
norteamericano**

2.

la música

1. _____

2. _____

Unit 2 · Getting Acquainted — Vocabulary

LESSON 1 · Greetings

Adiós. *Goodbye.*
bien *fine*
Buenos días. *Good morning.*
Buenas noches. *Good evening./Good night.*
Buenas tardes. *Good afternoon.*
gracias *thank you*
¿Cómo está usted? *How are you?* (to ask an adult)
¿Cómo estás? *How are you?* (to ask a friend)
¿Cómo te llamas? *What's your name?*

Estoy... *I am . . .*
Hasta luego. *See you later.*
¡Hola! *Hello!*
mal *not well*
Me llamo... *My name is . . .*
muy *very*
regular *okay*
tú *you* (informal)
usted *you* (formal)
¿Y tú? *And you?*
yo *I*

LESSON 2 · Age

¿Cuántos años tiene? *How old is (he/she)?*
¿Cuántos años tienes? *How old are you?* (to ask a friend)
Tengo ... años. *I'm . . . years old.*
Tiene ... años. *He/She is . . . years old.*
veintiuno *twenty-one*
veintidós *twenty-two*
veintitrés *twenty-three*
veinticuatro *twenty-four*

veinticinco *twenty-five*
veintiséis *twenty-six*
veintisiete *twenty-seven*
veintiocho *twenty-eight*
veintinueve *twenty-nine*
treinta *thirty*
cuarenta *forty*
cincuenta *fifty*
sesenta *sixty*

LESSON 3 · Sports and Classes

el baloncesto *basketball*
el béisbol *baseball*
la clase de español *Spanish class*
la clase de inglés *English class*
el fútbol *soccer*
el fútbol norteamericano *football*
la geografía *geography*
la natación *swimming*

la tarea *homework*
el tenis *tennis*
el voleibol *volleyball*
Me gusta... *I like . . .*
no *no*
No me gusta... *I don't like . . .*
sí *yes*
¿Te gusta...? *Do you like . . . ?*

LESSON 4 · Music and Food

el chocolate *chocolate*
la comida china *Chinese food*
la comida italiana *Italian food*
la comida mexicana *Mexican food*
la ensalada *salad*
la fruta *fruit*

el jugo *juice*
la música clásica *classical music*
la música jazz *jazz music*
la música pop/rock *pop/rock music*
la pizza *pizza*

UNIT 2

UNIT 2 · Getting Acquainted **Review and Assessment**

¡Ven conmigo! and *Adelante* Resources
- *Interactive CD-ROM Tutor,* Disc 1

Materials you will need
- Vocabulary flashcards
- Drawing paper

Language and Culture Objectives

Students will

- show their knowledge of greetings, talking about likes and dislikes in Spanish
- show their knowledge of culture related to the Spanish-speaking world
- express their knowledge orally and in the form of an in-class project

Review

1. Have students count to 60 as a class.
2. Call out food, music, sport, or school vocabulary and have students hold up the correct flashcard.
3. Have students ask a partner ¿**Cómo estás?** The partner makes an appropriate face to show that he/she understands the answer he/she gives.
4. Have students ask and answer the question ¿**Cuántos años tienes?** in pairs.
5. Have students ask their partners ¿**Te gusta...?** questions about food, music, school, and sports.

Assessment Options

Written

- Have students complete **¡Ya lo sé!,** Unit 2. You will find the script for the listening activity on page 113 of this guide.

- *Project* Have students make a poster describing themselves. Have them include the phrases to tell their name, their age, and several of their likes and dislikes. Have students illustrate their likes and dislikes and label them in Spanish.

Oral

1. Ask the student ¿**Cómo estás?**
2. Place five picture vocabulary flashcards on the desk for the student to identify.
3. Ask the student ¿**Cuántos años tienes?**
4. Ask the student ¿**Te gusta...?** and name a sport or a food.
5. Ask the student ¿**Te gusta...?** and name a type of music.
6. Ask the student to name a sport played in Spanish-speaking countries.

CD-ROM

- Use *Interactive CD-ROM Tutor,* Disc 1, Chapter 1, Activity 6, to assess students on categorizing sports, school, food, and music vocabulary.

UNIT 2

UNIT 2 · Getting Acquainted   ¡Ya lo sé!   Total Points: 40

A. Likes and dislikes

Look at the pictures and listen to what people like or don't like. If the sentence agrees with the drawing, write **sí.** If not, write **no.** (10 points)

1. _____

2. _____

3. _____

4. _____

5. _____

SCORE [____]

B. La quinceañera

Answer the following questions about **quinceañera** celebrations. (4 points)

1. Guadalupe's parents are throwing a **quinceañera** party for her on Saturday.

   How old will she be? _____

2. Who traditionally gives the girl a special gift? Circle the correct letter.

   a. her brother   **c.** her neighbors

   b. her godparents   **d.** her maternal grandparents

SCORE [____]

UNIT 2 · Getting Acquainted   **¡Ya lo sé!**   *continued*

C. How old are you?

Look at the illustrations below. First write the question you would use to ask a friend how old he or she is. Then match the letter of the person with the sentence that describes how old he or she is. (16 points)

Question: ¿ _____ **?**

_____ **1.** Silvia tiene veinte años.   _____ **3.** Cristina tiene dos años.

_____ **2.** Leonardo tiene cuatro años.   _____ **4.** Rodolfo tiene catorce años.

SCORE [   ]

D. How are you?

Match each Spanish sentence with the correct facial expression. (10 points)

_____ **1.** Estoy muy bien.   _____ **4.** Estoy mal.

_____ **2.** Muy mal.   _____ **5.** Bien, gracias.

_____ **3.** Estoy regular.

SCORE [   ]

TOTAL SCORE [/40   ]

UNIT 3 · School   Lesson 1   School Supplies

¡Ven conmigo! and Adelante Resources
- *Teaching Transparencies 2-A and 2-1*
- *Video Program*, Chapter 2
- *Interactive CD-ROM Tutor*, Disc 1

Materials you will need
- Index cards
- Advertisements with pictures of school supplies
- Scissors, tape or glue

Language and Culture Objectives
Students will
- learn the names of school supplies in Spanish
- learn what school supplies Spanish-speaking students need to buy

Motivate
- Ask students what school supplies they buy for their classes. Which do they think students in Spanish-speaking countries would buy? (similar ones, many also buy uniforms and textbooks)

Teach
1. *Visual Learners* Use *Teaching Transparency 2-A* or *Teaching Transparency 2-1* to present vocabulary for school supplies.
2. *Kinesthetic Learners* Ask students to hold up their school supplies as you call out the names in Spanish. For example, you hold up a pen and say **Tengo un bolígrafo.** Students hold up their pens and repeat the words **un bolígrafo.**
3. *Culture* Show students the Chapter 2 **Panorama cultural** video in which Spanish-speaking students are interviewed about their school supplies. As a pre-viewing activity, model talking about school supplies you have and ask volunteers to say which supplies they have. As a post-viewing activity, ask students to compare what the students in the video need for school with what they need. (students in the video buy their own textbooks and uniforms)
4. *Language Learning* Tell students that creating flashcards is a good way to reinforce language learning. Have students create their own set by drawing a school supply on one side of an index card and writing the name of the school supply in Spanish on the other side. Have students practice using their flashcards with a partner to review vocabulary.
5. *Game* **¡Anda a pescar!** Divide students into groups of four. Have them use their four sets of flashcards as playing cards. Students play Go Fish® asking questions about their group members' cards. **¿Tienes papel? No, no tengo papel.** Have students cover the backs of their cards so other students can't read them.
6. *Writing* Have students use Activity Master 3.1 to practice vocabulary for school supplies.

Additional Practice
- *Listening* Show students the **De antemano** video for Chapter 2. Pause after Paco or Abuela says a school supply, and ask students to hold up their flashcard of the object and repeat the word. Have students use the *Interactive CD-ROM Tutor,* Disc 1, Chapter 2, Activity 1 to practice school supply vocabulary.
- *Project* Have students make **Para el colegio** collages by using drawings and magazine pictures of school supplies. Students title the collage and label each school supply in Spanish.

Close
- *Game* Divide the class into two teams. Have them play **Dibújalo** (Pictionary®), in which students from each team take turns drawing a school supply for their team to guess. Each time the team guesses an item within one minute, it gets a point.

UNIT 3

Activity Master 3.1   School Supplies

1 Eduardo and his friends made lists of the supplies they need for school this year. First read their lists. Then complete the statements that follow to show who needs each item.

EDUARDO	MIGUEL	LOLA	RAFAEL	ROSITA
una mochila un lápiz una regla	un libro una calculadora un bolígrafo	un diccionario papel un cuaderno	una mochila un libro una goma de borrar	una carpeta una goma de borrar una regla

1. _____ needs a backpack, a pencil, and a ruler.

2. _____ needs a dictionary, paper, and a notebook.

3. _____ needs a backpack, a book, and an eraser.

4. _____ needs a book, a calculator, and a pen.

5. _____ needs a folder, an eraser, and a ruler.

2 Complete this crossword puzzle by writing in the Spanish words for the items pictured below. The correct definite article is included for each item. No spaces will remain blank.

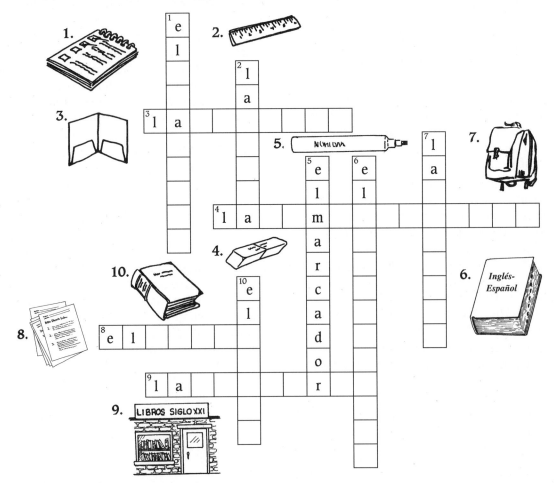

UNIT 3 · School   Lesson 2   Telling Time

¡Ven conmigo! and Adelante Resources
- *¡Ven conmigo! Annotated Teacher's Edition*
- *Adelante Annotated Teacher's Edition*
- *Interactive CD-ROM Tutor, Disc 1*

Materials you will need
- Flashcards of numbers 1–60
- Paper-plate clock
- Project: Paper plates, markers, construction paper, scissors, and brads

Language and Culture Objectives
Students will
- learn simple expressions for telling time in Spanish
- learn about going to school in the Spanish-speaking world

Motivate
- Ask students what numbers they would need to know in order to tell time. (1–59) To review, have each student count a number in sequence from one to 60 in Spanish. Then call out school supplies around the room for students to count.

Teach
1. **Visual Learners** Use a paper-plate clock to teach students to tell time and have students repeat the time after you. Begin with times on the hour 1–12, **¿Qué hora es? Es la una, son las dos...**, then proceed with quarter and half hours, **y cuarto, y media,** and **menos cuarto.**

2. **Language Learning** Tell students to practice these new Spanish phrases by telling themselves the time in Spanish when they look at a clock.

3. **TPR** Place large cut-out numbers from 1–12 in a circle on the floor to create a clock face. Have pairs of students sit or stand back to back in the center of the clock. Call out a time and have the students point their feet to the appropriate numbers.

4. **Kinesthetic Learners** Have students make paper-plate clocks by using brads to connect the hands of the clock to the plate. When they finish, call out times and have them move their clock hands to the correct position. Or, have them write the numbers 1–12, 15, 30, 45 and 00, to make a digital clock and have them assemble the correct numbers for the time.

5. **Group Work** Have students work in groups using their paper-plate clocks. One student arranges the hands and the other students take turns saying the time. Or the leader calls out a time and the group members move the hands of their clocks to the correct position.

6. **Writing** Have students complete Activity Master 3.2 to practice telling time.

Additional Practice
- **Listening** Have students use the *Interactive CD-ROM Tutor,* Disc 1, Chapter 3, Activity 2, to practice telling time.

- **Speaking** Have students work with a partner using their paper-plate clock or drawing digital times. One asks **¿Qué hora es?** and the other answers saying the time.

- **Game** Have students make **PONGA** cards with times written in the squares, including quarter and half hours. Call out times and have students mark their cards with scraps of paper. As in Bingo®, the first to connect 5 squares horizontally or vertically wins. See *¡Ven conmigo! Annotated Teacher's Edition* page 15C or *Adelante Annotated Teacher's Edition* page 19J for an example of a **PONGA** card.

- **Challenge** See **Enlaces,** pages 134–135 of *Adelante Annotated Teacher's Edition,* for information about time zones and the 24-hour clock.

Close
- **Game** Divide the class into two teams. Have one student from each team come to the board. Call out a time and have students write the numerals on the board. The first student to write it correctly earns one point for his or her team.

UNIT 3

Nombre _____ Clase _____ Fecha _____

 Activity Master 3.2   **Telling Time**

1 Valerie is spending Saturday afternoon working in her grandmother's clock store. In
Spanish, help Valerie catalog the new shipment by matching each clock to the correct time.

1. _____   3. _____

2. _____   4. _____

a. Son las once menos cuarto.

b. Son las cinco y media.

c. Es la una y ocho.

d. Son las cuatro y veinticinco.

2 Write the time in numerals in the box under each phrase.

Son las cuatro.   **Es la una.**   **Son las tres y cuarto.**   **Son las diez.**

3 Use the words in the vocabulary boxes to write the correct time under each watch.

Es la		dos		y cuarto
Son las		cinco		y media
		seis		menos cuarto
		siete		
		doce		

1. _____   2. _____   3. _____

_____   _____   _____

UNIT 3 · School   Lesson 3   Days of the Week

¡Ven conmigo! and Adelante Resources
- *Teaching Transparency 4-C*
- *Adelante Annotated Teacher's Edition*

Materials you will need
- Calendar in Spanish
- Drawing paper

Language and Culture Objectives
Students will
- learn the days of the week in Spanish
- learn to write the days in Spanish without capitalizing the first letter
- learn which day is often considered the first day of the week

Motivate
- Ask students why it would be important to know the days of the week as a visitor in a Spanish-speaking country.

Teach
1. *Listening* Model the pronunciation of each day as you write it on the board. Then erase **lunes** and ask students to supply the word for *Monday*. Next erase **martes** and have students give the first two days and repeat as you model the five remaining days.
2. *Kinesthetic Learners* Divide the class into seven groups and assign a day of the week to each. Have the groups stand in order Monday through Sunday. Ask each group **¿Qué día es?** Model the answer **Es el _____.** After asking the days in sequence, ask them in random order.
3. *Culture* Use *Teaching Transparency 4-C* to explain that in many Spanish-speaking countries, the calendar week begins on Monday. Is that the same or different than in the United States? (different) On what day of the week do calendars begin in the United States? (Sunday) Ask students what other difference they notice. (first letters are not capitalized)

4. *Writing* Have students use Activity Master 3.3 to review the days of the week.
5. *Visual Learners* Have students draw a picture of what they like to do on their favorite day of the week. Have them title the pictures in Spanish **Mi día favorito es _____.**

Additional Practice
- *Song* Put students in small groups. Have them choose a popular song and practice singing the days of the week to its tune.
- *Language Learning* Call out a day of the week in Spanish (for example, **miércoles**) and have the whole class give the days before and after (**martes, jueves**). This can also be done as a game by dividing the class into two teams and calling on individual students to supply the "before" and "after" days. If they do so correctly, they win a point for their team.
- *TPR* Randomly assign different days of the week to students by giving them each a piece of paper with a day of the week written on it. Then call out the days of the week, first in order, then randomly. Have students stand when their day of the week is called.
- *History* Teach the origins of the Spanish days of the week found in **Enlaces**, page 220 of *Adelante Annotated Teacher's Edition*.

Close
- *Game* Have students line up at the door before the end of class. Before the bell rings each student says one day of the week in sequence, beginning with Monday. Students who give the incorrect day go to the back of the line to try again.

UNIT 3

Nombre _____ Clase _____ Fecha _____

Activity Master 3.3   Days of the Week

1 Write the days of the week in Spanish in the six spaces provided. Remember not to capitalize the first letters of the days of the week.

JUNIO

a.	martes	b.	c.	d.	e.	f.
		1	2	3	4	5
6	7	8	9	10	11	12

a. _____   d. _____

b. _____   e. _____

c. _____   f. _____

What difference do you notice about which day begins the week in many Spanish-speaking countries? _____

_____

2 Unscramble these days of the week. Then use the blanks to the left to number the days in order.

MODELO   __1__ S U E L N _____ **LUNES** _____

_____ **a.** D Á S A O B _____

_____ **b.** U E J S E V _____

_____ **c.** C I É R M O S E L _____

_____ **d.** E R M A T S _____

_____ **e.** G I D O N O M _____

_____ **f.** E R I N S V E _____

30 Holt Spanish Exploratory Guide   Unit 3, Lesson 3

Copyright © by Holt, Rinehart and Winston. All rights reserved.

Teacher's Name _____ Class _____ Date _____

¡*Ven conmigo!* and *Adelante* Resources	Materials you will need
• *Teaching Transparency 3-A* • *Video Program,* Chapter 3 • *Interactive CD-ROM Tutor,* Disc 1	• Magazines • Poster board • Scissors

Language and Cultural Objectives
Students will
- learn the names of school subjects
- be able to say what their classes are
- be able to say when their classes are
- learn about school schedules in the Spanish-speaking world

Motivate
- Ask students what subjects they study. Which is their favorite? Ask students what they think it would be like to attend a school in a Spanish-speaking country.

Teach
1. *Visual Learners* Show students *Teaching Transparency 3-A* on school subjects and say the vocabulary aloud as students repeat after you. Have students raise their hands when you call out subjects they have.
2. *Culture* Show students the Chapter 3 **De antemano** on the video in which Claudia gets her school schedule. Pause on the close-up of her schedule. Go over the classes she takes. Then ask students which classes they have in common with her. How are their schedules different?
3. *Visual Learners* Have students make posters with pictures representing the classes they have. They draw a picture or clip one from a magazine to represent each class and label each in Spanish. Display *Teaching Transparency 3-A* to give students ideas for images to illustrate each subject.
4. *Kinesthetic Learners* Have students point to the pictures on their posters of school

subjects from the preceding activity as you talk about classes they have. (**¿Quién tiene geografía? Yo tengo...**)
5. *Visual/Auditory Learners* Use *Teaching Transparency 3-A* to present how to talk about when classes begin. Start with Spanish class, saying **¿A qué hora es la clase de español? A las...** Have students repeat after you. Talk about your class schedule or the schedule of an imaginary student. Then proceed involving students in questions about their schedules.
6. *Writing* Have students use Activity Master 3.4 to practice vocabulary for school subjects.

Additional Practice
- *Speaking* Have pairs ask each other about classes **¿Tienes matemáticas? Sí, tengo matemáticas.** Use *Teaching Transparency 3-A* on school subjects to ask students what they already have for each class: **¿Tienes un libro para la clase de inglés?** Have pairs of students ask each other what supplies they have for their classes.
- *Reading* Have students use the *Interactive CD-ROM Tutor,* Disc 1, Chapter 3, Activity 3, to practice vocabulary for school subjects.

Close
- *Game* **Dibújalo** Divide students into two teams. Have one student from each team come to the board to draw. Show both students a vocabulary word from Unit 3. As they draw, their teams guess what vocabulary word it could be. The team that guesses the word first wins a point. The team with more points wins.

UNIT 3

Activity Master 3.4

School Subjects

1 Use the pictures to fill in the classes that Ángela is taking this semester. Then rearrange the circled letters to find out what her favorite class is.

1.

g | | | ◯ | | |

2.

e | | | | ◯ | |

f | | ◯ | |

3.

c | | | | ◯ | | ◯ |

4.

m | | | | | | | | ◯ |

5.

a | | ◯ |

6.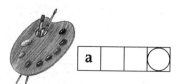

f | | | ◯ | |

What's her favorite class? ___ ___ ___ ___ ___ ___ ___ ___

2 Choose the class each book is for, based on its title.

_____ 1. *Fractions, Decimals, and Long Division*   **a.** la historia

_____ 2. *Elements of Literature*®   **b.** la computación

_____ 3. *¡Ven conmigo! Adelante*®   **c.** la educación física

_____ 4. *The United States Since Colonial Times*   **d.** el español

_____ 5. *Internet Technology*   **e.** las matemáticas

_____ 6. *Basketball Basics*®   **f.** el inglés

UNIT 3 · School   Vocabulary

LESSON 1 · School Supplies

el bolígrafo *ballpoint pen*
la calculadora *calculator*
la carpeta *folder*
el colegio *school*
el cuaderno *notebook*
el diccionario *dictionary*
la goma de borrar *eraser*
el lápiz *pencil*
la librería *bookstore*

el libro *book*
la mochila *backpack*
el papel *paper*
la regla *ruler*
el *the* (masculine)
la *the* (feminine)
un *a* (masculine)
una *a* (feminine)

LESSON 2 · Telling Time

A las... *At . . . o'clock*
Es la una. *It's one o'clock.*
de la mañana *in the morning* (A.M.)
de la noche *in the evening* (P.M.)
de la tarde *in the afternoon* (P.M.)
¿Qué hora es? *What time is it?*
Son las... *It's . . . o'clock.*
menos cuarto *quarter to (the hour)*

y cuarto *quarter past (the hour)*
y media *half past (the hour)*
veinte *twenty*
treinta *thirty*
cuarenta *forty*
cincuenta *fifty*
sesenta *sixty*

LESSON 3 · Days of the Week

lunes *Monday*
martes *Tuesday*
miércoles *Wednesday*
jueves *Thursday*
viernes *Friday*

sábado *Saturday*
domingo *Sunday*
¿Qué día es? *What day is it?*
Es el... *It's . . .*

LESSON 4 · School Subjects

A las... *At . . .*
¿A qué hora...? *At what time . . . ?*
el almuerzo *lunch*
el arte *art*
las ciencias *science*
las ciencias sociales *social sciences*
la computación *computer science*

la educación física *physical education*
el español *Spanish*
el francés *French*
la geografía *geography*
la historia *history*
el inglés *English*
las matemáticas *mathematics*

Teacher's Name _____ Class _____ Date _____

UNIT 3 · School   Review and Assessment

¡Ven conmigo! and *Adelante* Resources
- *Interactive CD-ROM Tutor,* Disc 1

Materials you will need
- Paper-plate clocks
- School supplies
- Drawing paper

Language and Culture Assessment Objectives

Students will
- show their knowledge of school-related vocabulary in Spanish
- show their knowledge of culture related to school subjects
- express their knowledge orally and in the form of an in-class project

Review

1. Have students count to 20 in Spanish as a class. Have students count the number of different school supplies in the room (for example, rulers or backpacks).
2. Call out times and have students set the hands of their paper-plate clocks to that time.
3. Have students say the days of the week. Have one student start with **lunes**, the next continue with **martes**, and so on. Cycle through the days as many times as necessary to have each student participate.
4. Have students ask and tell each other what classes they have: **¿Tienes...?**
5. Lead a discussion about the similarities and differences between what students buy to get ready for school in Spanish-speaking countries and what they buy. (general supplies, books, uniforms)

Assessment Options

Written
- Have students complete **¡Ya lo sé!**, Unit 3. You will find the script for the listening activity on page 113 of this guide.
- *Project* Have students work on a class schedule project, **Mi horario escolar**. The schedules should include the days of the week, the times of class periods, and at least five class subjects.

Oral
1. Place five different school supplies on the student's desk for the student to identify.
2. Hold up a clock and ask the student **¿Qué hora es?**
3. Ask the student **¿Qué día es?** and have the student tell you the day of the week.
4. Ask the student about the classes he or she has: **¿Tienes geografía?**
5. Ask the student to name the days he or she takes Spanish.

CD-ROM
- Use *Interactive CD-ROM Tutor,* Disc 1, Chapter 2 Activity 1, Chapter 3 Activity 2, and Chapter 3 Activity 3, to have students review school supply vocabulary, telling time, and school subject vocabulary.

UNIT 3 · School   ¡Ya lo sé!   **Total Points: 40**

A. School Supplies

Listen as Clara talks about what she has or doesn't have in her backpack. Look at the drawings and decide, based on what you hear, if the items are in the backpack or not. Circle **sí** or **no** for each item below. (10 points)

1. sí no

4. sí no

2. sí no

5. sí no

3. sí no

SCORE [   ]

B. Telling Time

Match the watches below with the correct time. (9 points)

a

b

c

_____ 1. Son las cuatro y media.

_____ 2. Son las cuatro y cuarto.

_____ 3. Son las doce menos cuarto.

SCORE [   ]

UNIT 3

UNIT 3 · School   ¡Ya lo sé!   *continued*

C. School Subjects

Below is Armando's class schedule. Fill in the blanks with the correct letters of the classes he's taking. Use the drawings as clues. (14 points)

8:00	*Elements of Literature*	1. _____
9:00	2/4 x 5/10 = 1/4	2. _____
10:00		3. _____
11:00		4. _____
1:00		5. _____
2:00		6. _____
3:00	¡Hola!	7. _____

a. las matemáticas

b. el español

c. las ciencias

d. la computación

e. el inglés

f. la educación física

g. el arte

SCORE _____

D. Days of the Week

Which of the following words is *not* a day of the week? Place an X on the line next to the item that is not a day of the week. (5 points)

_____ 1. sábado   _____ 4. jueves   _____ 7. lunes

_____ 2. martes   _____ 5. miércoles   _____ 8. jóvenes

_____ 3. viernes   _____ 6. domingo

SCORE _____

E. ¿Qué día es?

Write a number one on the line next to the day in the activity above that is the first day of the week in many Spanish-speaking countries. (2 points)

SCORE _____

TOTAL SCORE _____ /40

UNIT 4 · Sports and Pastimes   Lesson 1   Sports

¡Ven conmigo! and Adelante/En camino Resources

- *Teaching Transparency 1-B*
- *En camino Annotated Teacher's Edition*

Materials you will need

- Unit 2 sport vocabulary cards
- Magazine pictures of sports
- Drawing paper and markers

Language and Culture Objectives

Students will

- learn cultural information about baseball
- learn phrases to invite people to play sports

Motivate

- Ask students how many of them play baseball and softball. Tell students that in this unit they will learn to ask friends to play sports and take part in other pastimes.

Teach

1. *Culture* Baseball is a very popular sport in Latin America, especially in the Caribbean. Every February, teams from Puerto Rico, Venezuela, Mexico, and the Dominican Republic play in a winter baseball championship called the Caribbean Series. Cuba's baseball team defeated the United States' team to win the gold medal in baseball in the 1996 Olympic Games. Baseball teams from the U.S. recruit many Latin American players. What Latin American baseball players can students name? (Ramón Martínez, Sandy Alomar, Wilson Álvarez, among others)

2. *Visual Learners* Review sports vocabulary with *Teaching Transparency 1-B*. Have students repeat the names of the sports after you. Then introduce **Me gustaría jugar al...** and **No me gustaría jugar al...** to talk about sports you would like and would not like to play. Use the new phrases to quiz students about sports vocabulary. For example, say **Me gustaría jugar al fútbol** and have students hold up their picture flashcard from Unit 2 for soccer. Or, show a magazine picture of the sport instead of saying the word and have students say the word aloud. For example, say **Me gustaría...** as you hold up a picture of a tennis player. Students say **jugar al tenis.**

3. *Kinesthetic Learners* Have students play charades with a partner. One partner mimes the action for a sport. The other partner then invites him or her to play that sport. For example, one partner mimes a soccer kick motion and the other asks **¿Te gustaría jugar al fútbol?** Then the partners switch roles. Each student mimes two sports.

4. *Listening* To play the game **PONGA**, first write the vocabulary for sports on the board. Have students draw a Bingo® card that is five squares by five squares and write **libre** *(free)* in the center square. Then students draw a picture of one of the six sports in this lesson in each square, for example, a tennis racket or a soccer ball. Each sport will be represented several times. Begin play by saying several sentences or questions about the six sports. Have students cover a square for the sport you say, for example, **¿Te gustaría jugar al tenis?** The first student to link five squares vertically, diagonally, or horizontally calls out **PONGA.**

5. *Writing* Have students use Activity Master 4.1 to practice phrases to talk about sports they would or would not like to play.

Additional Practice

- *Culture* Present **Enlaces** about baseball in Latin America, on pages 236–237 of *En camino*.

- *Project* Have students draw a three-frame cartoon of two friends inviting each other to play sports.

Close

- *Game* Have students use their **PONGA** cards as interviewing tools. They circulate around the classroom asking their classmates if they like to play particular sports. If the classmate likes the sport, the interviewer writes an "○" on the card and if the classmate doesn't like it, he or she writes an "×." The classmate then signs his or her initials on the card. As in tic-tac-toe, the first student to link five ×'s or ○'s vertically, diagonally, or horizontally wins.

Activity Master 4.1 Sports

1 Match the statement or question about the sport with the correct drawing.

a

b

c

_____ 1. No me gustaría jugar al fútbol norteamericano.

_____ 2. ¿Te gustaría jugar al baloncesto?

_____ 3. Me gustaría jugar al tenis.

2 Combine words from the two vocabulary boxes to tell whether or not you like these sports.

Me gusta		jugar al tenis
No me gusta		jugar al fútbol
		jugar al voleibol

1

2

3

1. _____

2. _____

3. _____

Unit 4 · Sports and Pastimes   Lesson 2   More Sports

UNIT 4

¡Ven conmigo! and *Adelante/En camino* Resources

- *Teaching Transparency 4-A*
- *Video Program,* Chapters 11 and 12, Location Opener

Materials you will need

- Transparency marker
- Magazine pictures or drawings of vocabulary items
- Clay or Play-Doh®
- Tape or glue

Language and Culture Objectives

Students will

- learn cultural information about skiing
- learn more sports vocabulary

Motivate

- Ask students what exercise they like to do. Tell them that they will learn how to ask friends in Spanish if they would like to do these activities.

Teach

1. *Culture*   Several Spanish-speaking countries have mountainous areas where people downhill ski. (Spain, Chile, and Argentina) Spain is Europe's second-most mountainous country after Switzerland. The Pyrenees Mountains, the natural border between France and Spain, are an excellent location for downhill skiing and other winter sports. The Andes Mountains of South America are the highest mountains outside Asia.

2. *Visual Learners*   Display *Teaching Transparency 4-A.* Write the words for the sports covered in this lesson on the transparency as you present the vocabulary aloud. Play the Location Opener video for Chapters 11 and 12 about Puerto Rico for students. Ask them what they would like to do in Puerto Rico if their family traveled there, for example, ¿**Te gustaría nadar?**

3. *Listening*   Clip pictures from magazines or draw new vocabulary items and mount them on cards. Then randomly number them. As you say the Spanish word for a vocabulary image, students say its number in Spanish. Once they are familiar with the words, the students can say the Spanish words for each image as you cue them by stating the number.

4. *Tactile Learners*   Divide students into two or four teams to play **Fórmalo.** Give a ball of clay or Play-Doh® to each group. Show a vocabulary word to one student from each team. Without telling their team the word, they sculpt equipment related to the sport or a person playing the sport. The first team to guess the sport their group member is sculpting wins a point.

5. *Speaking*   Introduce **mucho, para nada,** and **un poco.** Have students work individually to write a sports survey. Each student writes three questions to ask a partner. They write questions using the vocabulary from this lesson and three sports from the previous lesson. Then they ask their partner the questions, for example, ¿**Te gusta montar en bicicleta?** Their partner will respond in full sentences saying how much he or she likes or doesn't like something, for example, **No me gusta para nada montar en bicicleta.** Then the partners switch roles.

6. *Writing*   Have students complete Activity Master 4.2 to practice new sports vocabulary.

Additional Practice

- *Project*   Have students draw or clip pictures from magazines of people doing four of the sports from this lesson in a park or on an exercise trail. Ask students to label each sport.

Close

- *Game*   **Charades** Divide the class into two teams for students to play charades. Appoint one student as the timekeeper. With a time limit of two or three minutes, a student from one group mimes a sport while his or her group guesses which it is. The teams take turns. The team with the lower time score wins. Students can also vote on the most realistic mime, the funniest mime, etc.

UNIT 4

Activity Master 4.2   **More Sports**

1 Match the drawing with the correct statement or question. Write the letter of the drawing in the space provided.

    ⓐ   **ⓑ**   **ⓒ**   **ⓓ**

_____ 1. No me gusta para nada esquiar.   _____ 3. Me gusta un poco correr.

_____ 2. Me gusta mucho nadar.   _____ 4. ¿Te gusta patinar en línea?

2 You and your family have just won a free vacation at a beach resort in Mexico. Write the letter of the sport symbol next to the question about it. Then check **sí** or **no** to say if you would like to do the activity during your vacation.

    ⓐ   **ⓑ**   **ⓒ**   **ⓓ**   **ⓔ**

Picture	Survey Question	Sí	No
	1. ¿Te gustaría jugar al tenis?		
	2. ¿Te gustaría montar en bicicleta?		
	3. ¿Te gustaría jugar al voleibol?		
	4. ¿Te gustaría bailar?		
	5. ¿Te gustaría jugar al fútbol?		

Unit 4 · Sports and Pastimes — Lesson 3 — Pastimes

¡Ven conmigo! and Adelante Resources
- *Teaching Transparencies 4-A* and *4-B*
- *Video Program,* Chapter 4

Materials you will need
- Index cards
- Magazines, scissors
- Tape or glue
- Shoebox for each student
- Construction paper

Language and Culture Objectives
Students will
- learn cultural information about the **paseo**
- learn phrases to talk about pastimes

Motivate
- Ask students what they like to do in their free time. Tell them they will learn to talk about their pastimes and to ask others to do free-time activities in this lesson.

Teach
1. *Culture* The **paseo** is a tradition in Spanish-speaking countries. People of all ages stroll around the **plaza** or along the streets of a town in the evening to socialize, and to see people and be seen. Friends or families walk, talk, and greet others. Play the Chapter 4 video **Panorama cultural** interviews in which young people talk about **paseo** customs.
2. *Visual Learners* Display *Teaching Transparencies 4-A* and *4-B* to present pastime vocabulary. Cover the words not included in the vocabulary list on page 45.
3. *Language Learning* Have students make picture flashcards of the vocabulary from this lesson. On an index card they may draw or paste pictures clipped from magazines and write the word in Spanish on the other side of the card. Have students use their flashcards to practice the new vocabulary with a partner.
4. *Listening* Talk about what you like to do in your free time after school, for example, **Me gusta tocar la guitarra después de las clases.** Have students hold up their corresponding picture flashcard.
5. *Writing* Have students use Activity Master 4.3 to practice vocabulary for free-time activities.

Additional Practice
- *Kinesthetic Learners* Divide the class into two teams. Have students play charades to practice vocabulary for pastimes.
- *Project* Have students make shadow boxes of their pastimes. Students may choose to depict one to three of their favorite activities using drawings or pictures clipped from magazines. They glue or tape the images inside shoe boxes to make a miniature scene of free-time activities.

Close
- *Game* **Dibújalo** Divide the class into two teams. Have a student from one group draw a pastime on the board while his or her group guesses which it is. The teams alternate turns. The team that guesses the most words correctly, wins.

Activity Master 4.3   **Pastimes**

UNIT 4

1 Write the letter of the picture next to the sentence it matches.

_____ 1. Me gusta tocar la guitarra.

_____ 2. Me gusta tocar el piano.

_____ 3. Me gusta estudiar.

ⓐ   ⓑ   ⓒ

2 Write four sentences about what you like to do in your free time. Use the phrases given.

MODELO   **Me gusta jugar a los videojuegos.**

> **jugar a los videojuegos**   **cantar**   **hablar por teléfono**
> **pasar el rato con amigos**   **mirar la televisión**
> **escuchar música**   **leer**   **tocar el piano**   **dibujar**

1. _____

2. _____

3. _____

4. _____

3 Your friend has passed you a note in the hall asking what you want to do tomorrow. Write a complete answer to each question, using **mucho, un poco,** or **para nada.**

MODELO   **¿Te gustaría cantar mañana?**
                     —Sí, me gustaría un poco. or **—No, no me gustaría para nada.**

1. ¿Te gustaría escuchar música mañana? _____

_____

2. ¿Te gustaría mirar la televisión mañana? _____

_____

3. ¿Te gustaría jugar a los videojuegos mañana? _____

_____

Unit 4 · Sports and Pastimes   Lesson 4   Describing Activities

¡Ven conmigo! and Adelante Resources
- *Teaching Transparencies 1-B, 4-A, 4-B*
- *Interactive CD-ROM Tutor*, Disc 1

Materials you will need
- Index cards
- Markers
- Drawing paper

Language and Culture Objectives

Students will
- learn about how Hispanic teens often spend Sundays
- learn words to describe activities

Motivate
- Ask students to describe why they like their favorite sport or pastimes. Tell them that in this lesson they will learn to describe why they like their favorite activities.

Teach
1. *Culture*   Discuss with students the tradition in Spain and Latin America of spending Sundays with the family. Hispanic teens in the United States often spend Sundays with their families as well. Ask students how they generally spend Sundays. Do they sleep late? go to the park? visit grandparents? Do they have fun or is it boring?

2. *Visual Learners*   Display *Teaching Transparencies 1-B, 4-A,* and *4-B*. Model phrases for giving opinions about the sports and pastimes on the transparencies, for example, **No me gusta correr. Es muy difícil.**

3. *Listening*   Write these names and activities on the board and have students write them in their notebooks: **1) Patricia — escuchar música; 2) Marcelino — tocar la guitarra;**

3) **Ángela — mirar la televisión; 4) Samuel — dibujar.** Write these adjectives in a box: **divertido, interesante, fácil.** Read the following script and have students write the adjective for each person's opinion they hear. **1) Me llamo Patricia. Me gusta escuchar música porque es *divertido.* 2) Me llamo Marcelino. Me gusta tocar la guitarra porque es *interesante.* 3) Me llamo Ángela. Me gusta mirar la televisión porque es *fácil.* 4) Me llamo Samuel. Me gusta dibujar porque es *divertido.***

4. *Writing*   Have students practice writing their opinions in Spanish using Activity Master 4.4.

Additional Practice
- *Project 1*   Have students draw a cartoon of themselves and three friends or family members. Students write a speech bubble for each person. The speech bubble says what the person likes to do and why. For example, the speech bubble for a friend might read: **Me gusta patinar en línea porque es divertido.**

Close
- *Project 2*   Have students make a poster of their opinions. They divide the paper into four squares. In each square they write an adjective, for example, **divertido, aburrido, interesante,** and **horrible.** They draw a picture of an activity under each category, labeling the activity in Spanish. They label the poster **Mis opiniones.**

Nombre _____ Clase _____ Fecha _____

UNIT 4

1 Using the words in the boxes, write your opinion about the activities pictured.
Write whether or not you like each one and why. Follow the **modelo**.

MODELO   **No me gusta mirar la televisión porque es aburrido.**

Me gusta
No me gusta

interesante
divertido
difícil
fácil
horrible

        nadar   **esquiar**   **patinar en línea**

1. _____ porque es _____.

2. _____ porque es _____.

3. _____ porque es _____.

2 Choose which opinion fits each person pictured. Write the letter of the opinion in the blank
provided.

_____ 1. ¿Te gusta bailar, Marco?

    a. No, porque es difícil.

    b. Sí, porque es divertido.

_____ 2. ¿Te gusta jugar al fútbol, Carmen?

    a. Sí, porque es interesante.

    b. No. Me gusta jugar al béisbol.

_____ 3. ¿Te gusta pasar el rato con amigos, Luisa?

    a. No, porque es aburrido.

    b. Sí, porque es divertido.

Unit 4 · Sports and Pastimes   Vocabulary

UNIT 4

LESSON 1 · Sports

¿Te gustaría...? *Would you like to . . . ?*
Me gustaría... *I would like to . . .*
jugar al... *to play (a sport)*

el baloncesto *basketball*
el béisbol *baseball*
el fútbol *soccer*
el fútbol norteamericano *football*
el tenis *tennis*
el voleibol *volleyball*

LESSON 2 · More Sports

bailar *to dance*
correr *to run*
esquiar *to ski*
hacer monopatín *to skateboard*
montar en bicicleta *to ride a bike*

nadar *to swim*
patinar en línea *to in-line skate*
mucho *a lot*
un poco *a little*
para nada *not at all*

LESSON 3 · Pastimes

cantar *to sing*
dibujar *to draw*
escuchar música *to listen to music*
estudiar *to study*
hablar por teléfono *to talk on the phone*
jugar a los videojuegos *to play videogames*

leer *to read*
mirar la televisión *to watch TV*
pasar el rato con amigos *to spend time with friends*
tocar el piano *to play the piano*
tocar la guitarra *to play the guitar*

LESSON 4 · Describing Activities

Es... *It's . . .*
  aburrido *boring*
  difícil *difficult*
  divertido *fun*

fácil *easy*
interesante *interesting*
horrible *horrible*
porque *because*

Unit 4 · Sports and Pastimes   Review and Assessment

UNIT 4

¡Ven conmigo! and Adelante Resources
- *Interactive CD-ROM Tutor,* Disc 1

Materials you will need
- Vocabulary flashcards
- Magazines
- Drawing paper or poster board

Language and Culture Assessment Objectives

Students will

- show their knowledge of sports and pastime vocabulary in Spanish
- show their knowledge of culture related to the Spanish-speaking world
- express their knowledge orally and in the form of an in-class project

Review

1. Ask students to name several sports that are popular in Spanish-speaking countries. Also ask them to name some common weekend activities for Hispanic teenagers.

2. Call out a sport or pastime and have students hold up the correct flashcard.

3. Have students ask their partners ¿Te gusta...? questions about sports and pastimes. Have them answer using adjectives to explain why they like that sport or pastime.

Assessment Options

Written

- Have students complete ¡Ya lo sé!, Unit 4. You will find the script for the listening activity on page 114 of this guide.

- *Project* Have students make a poster of their pastimes called **Mi tiempo libre.** Students may draw the activities or clip pictures of them from magazines. They use these to make a poster of five to eight pastimes and write a label for each in Spanish.

Oral

1. Ask the student ¿**Te gustaría patinar en línea después de las clases?**

2. Ask the student ¿**Te gustaría estudiar después de las clases?**

3. Place five picture vocabulary flashcards of sports and pastimes on the desk for the student to identify.

4. Ask the student ¿**Te gusta jugar al...?** and name a sport.

5. Ask the student ¿**Te gusta...?** and name a pastime.

6. Ask the student to name a Spanish-speaking country where many people go skiing. (Spain, Chile, or Argentina)

CD-ROM

- Use the *Interactive CD-ROM Tutor,* Disc 1, Chapter 1, Activity 6, to review sports.

Nombre _____ Clase _____ Fecha _____

A. Invitations

Listen as four teens respond to invitations to play sports or do free-time activities. Match the pictures below with the five statements you hear. (10 points)

a

b

c

d

e

1. _____   3. _____   5. _____

2. _____   4. _____

SCORE [ ]

B. El Paseo

Circle the letter of the best answer to each of the following questions. (8 points)

1. Which statement best describes what **paseo** means?

   a. a special Argentinean mountain festival

   b. a tradition of walking and socializing

   c. a custom of a light snack in the afternoons

2. Which of the following people participate in the **paseo**?

   a. teenagers

   b. older people

   c. people of all ages

SCORE [ ]

Unit 4 · Sports and Pastimes　　　**¡Ya lo sé!**　　　*continued*

UNIT 4

C. Pastimes

Match the picture with the statement the person in the picture would most likely make.
Write the correct letter in the space provided. (10 points)

a　　　　**b**　　　　**c**　　　　**d**　　　　**e**

_____ 1. Me gusta jugar al tenis con Federico.

_____ 2. Me gusta correr con mi amiga Carolina.

_____ 3. ¿Te gusta esquiar?

_____ 4. Me gusta pasar el rato con amigos.

_____ 5. Me gustaría jugar al baloncesto.

SCORE _____

D. Opinions

Your Costa Rican pen pal wants to know more about you. Write your
answers to the following four questions. Make sure to tell why you
like or don't like the activity and use a different adjective for each.
Use the adjectives in the box. (12 points)

> divertido　aburrido
> interesante　difícil
> fácil　horrible

MODELO　　　**¿Te gusta tocar el piano?**
　　　　　　　Sí, me gusta tocar el piano porque es divertido.

1. ¿Te gusta nadar? _____

2. ¿Te gusta estudiar? _____

3. ¿Te gusta jugar a los videojuegos? _____

4. ¿Te gusta hablar por teléfono? _____

SCORE _____

TOTAL SCORE _____ /40

UNIT 5 · Weather and Seasons   Lesson 1   Weather

¡Ven conmigo! and Adelante Resources
- *Teaching Transparency 5-C* and *Map 4*
- *Adelante Annotated Teacher's Edition*
- *Video Program,* Chapter 5 and *Guide*
- *Interactive CD-ROM Tutor,* Disc 2

Materials you will need
- Index cards
- Magazines
- Tape or glue, scissors
- Transparency marker

Language and Culture Objectives
Students will
- learn cultural information about the tropics
- learn phrases to talk about weather

Motivate
- Ask students what kind of weather they like best. Tell them they will learn to talk about the weather in this lesson.

Teach
1. *Culture* Some Spanish-speaking people live in tropical areas. Tropical climates affect every aspect of people's clothing, houses, and food. Houses in Central America, for example, in Guatemala, often have open patios in the center that are used as living rooms, to wash and dry laundry, or to grow decorative plants. Windows may be permanently open to the outside to allow breezes to pass through. In the tropics, houses don't need central heating because the weather rarely gets cold. Winters are rainy rather than snowy. Fresh fruits are readily available and inexpensive all year round, since fruit may be grown in all four seasons.

2. *Visual Learners* Show students *Teaching Transparency 5-C* to introduce expressions to talk about the weather. Say the expressions out loud as you point to the pictures and have students repeat them after you.

3. *Listening* List the cities and states mentioned in the weather report in the Chapter 5 video. Number them one to five. Write weather vocabulary words on the board and letter them *a* through *e*. (**a. Hace frío. b. Está nevando. c. Está lloviendo. d. Hace sol. Hace mucho calor. e. Hace viento.**) Play the weather report found in the Chapter 5 video

dramatic episode. Have students match the weather with the city where it is reported.

4. *Language Learning* Have students make picture flashcards of the weather expressions from this lesson. Students attach a picture they have drawn, or one from a magazine, on one side of an index card and write the word in Spanish on the other side.

5. *Speaking* Write the question ¿**Qué tiempo hace?** on the board. In pairs, have students use their picture flashcards as prompts to answer their partner's question ¿**Qué tiempo hace?**

6. *Writing* Have students complete Activity Master 5.1 to practice writing weather expressions.

Additional Practice
- *Science Link* Use the information from **Enlaces** in *Adelante,* page 221, to talk about tracking hurricanes on a map. Draw graph lines on *Map Transparency 4* of the Caribbean with a transparency marker. Use the lines to track the latitude and longitude of Hurricane Hortense and Hurricane Dolly on the overhead. Ask students which countries these hurricanes hit. (Dominican Republic, Puerto Rico and Mexico)

- *Visual Learners* Have students practice weather vocabulary with Disc 2, Chapter 5, Activity 5 of the *Interactive CD-ROM Tutor.*

- *Project* Have students keep a five-day weather diary during Unit 5. They write the five weekdays and the weather conditions for each day in Spanish.

Close
- *Game* Divide the class into two teams for **Dibújalo** (Pictionary®). Have students draw pictures to represent weather expressions.

UNIT 5

Activity Master 5.1   Weather

1 It's Julio's first day as a weather forecaster and he's arrived late! Help him get ready for the broadcast by matching the weather descriptions in the word box with the weather condition listed for the cities below.

> Hace frío.   Hace mucho calor.   Hace sol.
>
> Está lloviendo.   Hace viento.
>
>   Está nevando.   Hace fresco.   Está nublado.

_____   1. a windy day in Chicago

_____   2. a snowy evening in Aspen

_____   3. a cool morning in Boston

_____   4. a very hot afternoon in Santa Fe

_____   5. a cold morning in Anchorage

_____   6. a rainy afternoon in Seattle

_____   7. a cloudy evening in New York

_____   8. a bright sunny day in San Diego

2 Complete the sentences describing the weather in the following cities. Use the pictures below as clues.

    Phoenix   San Francisco   Minneapolis

1. En Phoenix _____.

2. En San Francisco _____.

3. En Minneapolis _____.

UNIT 5 · Weather and Seasons   Lesson 2   Months and Dates

¡Ven conmigo! and Adelante Resources
- *Audio Compact Discs, CD 5*
- *Listening Activities*

Materials you will need
- Transparency marker
- Calendars
- Flashcards for months of the year

Language and Culture Objectives
Students will
- learn cultural information about how dates are written in many Spanish-speaking countries
- learn phrases to talk about months and dates

Motivate
- Ask students to count from one to 31 in Spanish. Write the words on the board.

Teach
1. *Culture*   In many Spanish-speaking countries the date is written with the day first, then the month. For example, November 25 would be written 25/11. Ask students what date 4/2 would be in a Spanish-speaking country. (**el 4 de febrero**) Tell students that, like the days of the week, the months are not capitalized.

2. *Visual Learners*   Write the names of the months in Spanish on a transparency. Number them one to twelve in the margin. Say the names of the months and have students repeat after you. Then write the question **¿Cuál es la fecha?** on the board. Write the current date **Es el... de...** Have students repeat the new phrases after you. Give students additional examples of dates.

3. *Listening*   Play the song *Uno de enero* from Audio CD 5. See page 21 of the *Adelante Listening Activities*, or page 42 of the *¡Ven conmigo! Listening Activities*, for the lyrics. Have students sing along.

4. *Speaking*   Have students work in pairs. Using a page from a calendar, partners point to a date on the calendar and ask **¿Cuál es la fecha?** The other student will answer **Es el... de...** Have students switch roles after three questions.

5. *Listening*   Write the list of holidays on the board. Then say aloud the dates or months of the holidays and ask the class to identify them. After you have said all the dates, reverse the procedure. Point to the holidays on the board and let students match the dates with the holidays. 1. New Year's Eve; 2. New Year's Day; 3. Valentine's Day; 4. Lincoln's Birthday; 5. Spring Break; 6. April Fool's Day; 7. Mother's Day; 8. Independence Day; 9. Father's Day; 10. Thanksgiving; 11. Christmas; 12. Christmas Eve; a. **el primero de enero**; b. **el doce de febrero**; c. **el primero de abril**; d. **el cuatro de julio**; e. **el mes de mayo**; f. **el treinta y uno de diciembre**; g. **el catorce de febrero**; h. **el mes de marzo**; i. **el mes de junio**; j. **el veinticinco de diciembre**; k. **el mes de noviembre**; l. **el veinticuatro de diciembre**

6. *Writing*   Have students complete Activity Master 5.2 to practice writing the months and dates in Spanish.

Additional Practice
- *Project*   Have students make calendars of the current year or the year to come. Have students fill in the names of five holidays or other special days on their calendar.

Close
- *Game*   Put flashcards for months in chronological order, one on each of 12 desks in a row. Then have students stand next to the card that is the month of their birthday. Have students line up in order of the date of their birthdays. Students in each group ask one another **¿Cuál es la fecha de tu cumpleaños?** and answer **Es el...** to determine the sequence in which to line up. When the whole group is in order, have each student say the date of his or her birthday as they go down the line.

UNIT 5

Activity Master 5.2   Months and Dates

1 Unscramble the names of the months below. Write the words in the blanks that follow. Then number the months in the order they fall during the year.

_____ **a.** O N J U I _____

_____ **b.** B E R O F E R _____

_____ **c.** T A S G O O _____

_____ **d.** M E R P E S B I E T _____

_____ **e.** T U R O C E B _____

_____ **f.** N E O R E _____

_____ **g.** U J I L O _____

_____ **h.** M N O R I E B E V _____

_____ **i.** Z A R M O _____

_____ **j.** A Y M O _____

_____ **k.** R I E B C M I E D _____

_____ **l.** L I B A R _____

2 Match the following dates in English to their equivalent in Spanish. Write the letter in the space provided.

1. January 3 _____

2. March 31 _____

3. May 16 _____

4. August 9 _____

5. October 27 _____

6. December 6 _____

a. el nueve de agosto

b. el dieciséis de mayo

c. el veintisiete de octubre

d. el treinta y uno de marzo

e. el seis de diciembre

f. el tres de enero

3 Write the numbers for the following dates. Be sure to put the day first, then the month.

MODELO   **el tres de julio**   3/7

1. el veintiséis de julio _____

2. el veintisiete de febrero _____

3. el ocho de abril _____

4. el catorce de septiembre _____

5. el doce de noviembre _____

6. el diecinueve de junio _____

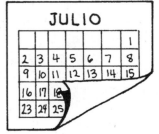

UNIT 5 · Weather and Seasons   Lesson 3   Seasons

¡Ven conmigo! and *Adelante* Resources
- *Teaching Transparency 5-B* and *Map Transparency 2*
- *Interactive CD-ROM Tutor,* Disc 2

Materials you will need
- Construction paper
- Markers or colored pencils
- Magazines, scissors, tape or glue

Language and Culture Objectives
Students will
- learn about the seasons in South America
- learn phrases to talk about the seasons
- learn how to talk about what they do and ask others what they do

Motivate
- Ask students what their favorite season is and why. Tell students they will learn to talk about the seasons, the months, and the weather associated with them in this unit.

Teach
1. *Culture* Display *Map Transparency 2.* Explain that the seasons in the southernmost part of South America are opposite to the seasons north of the equator. For example, in Chile, Argentina, and Uruguay, summer begins in December and winter begins in June. Ask students when would be a better time to go skiing in Chile, in December or in June. (June) When would be a good time to go to the beach? (December)

2. *Visual Learners* Display *Teaching Transparency 5-B* to teach students season vocabulary. Point to the season, say the word for it in Spanish, and have students repeat after you. Then point to the season and ask, **¿Qué estación es?** Students reply **Es...**

3. *Critical Thinking* Review how to talk about likes and dislikes. Ask volunteers to say they like to sing, dance, and swim. Write the phrases on the board. (**Me gusta cantar/bailar/nadar.**) Tell students they will learn how to say actions they do. For example, **Canto.** *(I sing.)*; **Bailo.** *(I dance.)*; **Nado.** *(I swim.)* Say the Spanish words out loud as you write them and have students repeat them after you. Ask students what the three

new sentences have in common. (they are made up of only one word, they end in -**o**) How are the action words different from the *I like* sentences? (they end in -**o**, not in -**ar**) Tell students to ask a friend *Do you swim in the summer?*, for example. They would say **¿Nadas en el verano?** Write it on the board, and have students repeat it after you. Then ask them to mime the action. How is **Nadas** different from **Nado**? (-**as** ending) Have students write down the sentences on the board. See Unit 4 for additional verbs that end in -**ar**.

4. *Listening* Read the following sentences aloud and have students mime the action. **En la primavera, camino. En el verano, nado. En el otoño, juego al fútbol americano. En el invierno, toco la guitarra.**

5. *Writing* Have students complete Activity Master 5.3 to practice writing the seasons and what they do in each season.

Additional Practice
- *Visual Learners* Have students use the *Interactive CD-ROM Tutor,* Disc 2, Chapter 5, Activity 5, to practice weather, months, and seasons.

- *Project* Have students make a poster of the seasons. Students fold a piece of construction paper twice to make four squares. They draw or clip pictures from magazines of the seasons and paste one in each square. Students label each square in Spanish with the name of the season and the name of the three months that make up the season. Then they draw an activity they do during each season and label it in Spanish.

Close
- *Game* Have students play **Dibújalo.** A student from one team draws the weather of one of the seasons and his or her team members guess which season it is.

U N I T 5

Activity Master 5.3　　　　　　　　　　　　　**Seasons**

1 Write what season it is for each picture below. Then, describe the weather in each picture.

> Hace mucho calor.　　Hace fresco.　　Hace sol.　　es la primavera　　Está nevando.
>
> 　　Hace viento.　　　es el verano　　　　　　　Está nublado.　　Hace frío.
>
> es el invierno　　　　　　　Está lloviendo.　　　　　　　　　es el otoño

1. En octubre _____. _____

2. En junio _____. _____

3. En abril _____. _____

4. En enero _____. _____

5. En marzo _____. _____

6. En julio _____. _____

2 Humberto took a survey about his classmates' favorite sports for each season but he dropped his papers and the answers got separated from the questions. Match Humberto's questions with his classmates' answers.

_____ 1. ¿Nadas en el verano?

_____ 2. ¿Juegas al baloncesto en el otoño?

_____ 3. ¿Patinas en línea en la primavera?

_____ 4. ¿Esquías en el invierno?

a. Sí, juego al baloncesto en el otoño.

b. No, no esquío en el invierno.

c. Sí, patino en línea en la primavera.

d. Sí, nado en el verano.

UNIT 5 · Weather and Seasons   Lesson 4   Holidays

¡Ven conmigo! and Adelante/En camino Resources

- *Teaching Transparency 10-A*
- *En camino Annotated Teacher's Edition*
- *Interactive CD-ROM Tutor*, Disc 3
- *Video Program*, Chapter 4

Materials you will need

- Index cards
- Magazines
- Tape or glue
- Tissue paper, pencils, scissors
- Posterboard, markers

Language and Culture Objectives

Students will

- learn cultural information about celebrations in Spanish-speaking countries
- learn phrases to talk about holidays

Motivate

- Ask students to talk about their favorite holidays. Ask them what makes the holiday special. Tell them they will learn the names of several holidays in Spanish in this unit.

Teach

1. *Culture*   In Mexico and in many other Latin American countries, it is common to have a **piñata** at a birthday party. A **piñata** is an object, or an animal, made of *papier mâché* and filled with treats. Everyone takes turns hitting the **piñata** with a stick until it breaks open and the treats fall on the ground. Then there is a wild scramble to gather up the treats.

2. *Visual Learners*   Display *Teaching Transparency 10-A* to introduce the names of holidays in Spanish. Point to the picture and say the name in Spanish aloud. Have students repeat the words after you. After students seem comfortable with the new phrases, ask about the dates of the holidays. For example, **¿Cuál es la fecha del Día de Independencia? (Es el cuatro de julio.)** Write the dates of the holidays on the board in Spanish and have students copy them down.

3. *Kinesthetic Learners*   Say the months aloud in Spanish. Have students stand and say **Mi cumpleaños** when you call their birthday month.

4. *Language Learning*   Have students make picture flashcards of holidays. Students draw or clip a picture from a magazine and paste it on one side of an index card and write the word in Spanish on the other side.

5. *Speaking*   In pairs, have students ask each other questions about the dates of holidays using **¿Cuál es la fecha de...?**

6. *Writing*   Have students use Activity Master 5.4 to practice holiday, month, and date vocabulary.

Additional Practice

- *Visual Learners*   Have students use the *Interactive CD-ROM Tutor*, Disc 3, Chapter 10, Activity 1, to practice vocabulary for holidays.

- *Project*   **Papel picado** is a Mexican folk art tradition of cutting tissue paper to make designs. To show students an example of how these decorations look, play the Chapter 4 video, **¿Dónde está María Inés? (a continuación)** of the visit to Taxco. Have students create their own **papel picado** designs. Tell students to fold the tissue paper in half twice. They then fold it in half once more to make a triangle. Students draw their designs on the triangle in pencil and carefully cut out the places they have marked with scissors. Alternative: Have students make a poster of their favorite holiday. Students draw their favorite part of the holiday, label the name of the holiday in Spanish, and write the date of the holiday in Spanish.

Close

- *Game*   State the date or month of a holiday and have students tell you the name of the holiday. For example, Teacher: **Es el 31 de diciembre.** Response: **la Nochevieja.**

Activity Master 5.4   Holidays

1 Write the dates of the following holidays and special occasions this year.

1. El Día de la Independencia   Es el _____.

2. El Día de Acción de Gracias   Es el _____.

3. El Día de los Enamorados   Es el _____.

4. El Año Nuevo   Es el _____.

5. Mi cumpleaños   Es el _____.

2 Answer the survey questions about what you like to do for the following holidays.

| la Nochevieja   el Día de los Enamorados <br> el Día de Acción de Gracias
     mi cumpleaños | comer   cantar <br> mirar la televisión
      bailar |

1. Para [___] _____ me gusta _____.

2. Para [___] _____ me gusta _____.

3. Para [___] _____ me gusta _____.

4. Para [___] _____ me gusta _____.

3 In Spanish, write the names of one or more holidays that are celebrated in the following months.

1. febrero _____

2. mayo _____

3. julio _____

4. noviembre _____

UNIT 5

Nombre _____ Clase _____ Fecha _____

LESSON 1 · Weather

¿Qué tiempo hace? *What's the weather like?*

Está lloviendo. *It's raining.*

Está nevando. *It's snowing.*

Está nublado. *It's cloudy.*

Hace buen tiempo. *The weather is nice.*

Hace (mucho) calor. *It's (very) hot.*

Hace fresco. *It's cool.*

Hace (mucho) frío. *It's (very) cold.*

Hace mal tiempo. *The weather is bad.*

Hace (mucho) sol. *It's (very) sunny.*

Hace (mucho) viento. *It's (very) windy.*

LESSON 2 · Months and Dates

¿Cuál es la fecha? *What is today's date?*

Es el... de... *It's the (date) of (month).*

el año *year*

el mes *month*

el primero *the first (of the month)*

enero *January*

febrero *February*

marzo *March*

abril *April*

mayo *May*

junio *June*

julio *July*

agosto *August*

septiembre *September*

octubre *October*

noviembre *November*

diciembre *December*

LESSON 3 · Seasons

las estaciones *seasons*

el invierno *winter*

el otoño *fall*

la primavera *spring*

el verano *summer*

¿Bailas? *Do you dance?*

Bailo. *I dance.*

¿Cantas? *Do you sing?*

Canto. *I sing.*

¿Juegas...? *Do you play . . . ?*

Juego... *I play . . .*

¿Nadas? *Do you swim?*

Nado. *I swim.*

LESSON 4 · Holidays

el Año Nuevo *New Year's Day*

el Día de Acción de Gracias *Thanksgiving Day*

el Día del Padre *Father's Day*

el Día de la Independencia *Independence Day*

el Día de las Madres *Mother's Day*

el Día de los Enamorados *Valentine's Day*

los días festivos *holidays*

la Navidad *Christmas*

la Nochebuena *Christmas Eve*

la Nochevieja *New Year's Eve*

las Pascuas *Easter*

mi cumpleaños *my birthday*

UNIT 5 · Weather and Seasons   Review and Assessment

¡Ven conmigo! and *Adelante* Resources
- *Interactive CD-ROM Tutor,* Disc 2

Materials you will need
- Vocabulary flashcards
- Drawing paper or butcher paper

Language and Culture Assessment Objectives

Students will

- show their knowledge of weather, seasons, months, and holiday vocabulary in Spanish
- show their understanding of cultural information about seasons and weather
- express their knowledge orally and in the form of an in-class project

Review

1. Have students recite the months in order in Spanish.
2. Call out a month, season, weather expression, or holiday and have students hold up the correct flashcard.
3. Have students ask and answer ¿**Qué tiempo hace?** in pairs.
4. Have students ask and tell each other ¿**Qué día es?** in pairs.

Assessment Options

Written
- Have students complete ¡**Ya lo sé!**, Unit 5. You will find the script for the listening activity on page 114 of this guide.

- *Project* Have students do a weather report. Begin by having each student draw a weather map of the United States on a large sheet of drawing paper or, if possible, butcher paper. Have them choose five different cities, decide what the weather is like in each city, and decorate the map accordingly. Then have students give a weather report in Spanish, using their map as a prop.

Oral

1. Point to a picture of weather and ask the student ¿**Qué tiempo hace?**
2. Place five picture vocabulary flashcards on the desk for the student to identify.
3. Ask the student ¿**Qué fecha es hoy?**
4. Ask the student ¿**Cuál es la fecha de tu cumpleaños?**
5. Name a holiday and ask the student to say its name in Spanish.
6. Ask the student to write a date in numerals the way a Spanish-speaker would. For example: **el cuatro de agosto** (4/8)

CD-ROM

- Have students use the *Interactive CD-ROM Tutor,* Disc 2, Chapter 5, Activity 5 to review weather, months, and seasons vocabulary and Disc 3, Chapter 10, Activity 1 to review holidays.

UNIT 5

UNIT 5 · Weather and Seasons   ¡Ya lo sé!   Total Points: 40

A. Weather

Listen to descriptions of the weather for various places. Match what you hear to the appropriate pictures below. (8 points)

a. spring

b. summer

c. fall

d. winter

1. _____   2. _____   3. _____   4. _____

SCORE [   ]

B. Holidays

Match the name of the holiday with the date when it occurs. Write the letter of the correct date on the line next to the holiday. (10 points)

_____ 1. La Navidad

_____ 2. El Día de los Enamorados

_____ 3. El Día de la Independencia

_____ 4. La Nochebuena

_____ 5. La Nochevieja

a. el veinticinco de diciembre

b. el treinta y uno de diciembre

c. el cuatro de julio

d. el catorce de febrero

e. el veinticuatro de diciembre

SCORE [   ]

UNIT 5 · Weather and Seasons   ¡Ya lo sé!   *continued*

C. Sports

Complete each sentence with the appropriate activity from
the word box. (16 points)

patino en línea   esquío

nado   juego al fútbol

1. En el invierno, _____ .

2. En la primavera, _____ .

3. En el verano, _____ .

4. En el otoño, _____ .

SCORE [   ]

D. Las fechas

The following two dates are written in the style of most Spanish-speaking countries. Match
the dates written in numbers with the dates written in words. (6 points)

1. 6/2 _____

2. 24/6 _____

a. el dos de junio

b. el veinticuatro de junio

c. el seis de febrero

SCORE [   ]

TOTAL SCORE [   ] /40

UNIT 6 · Food and Beverages   Lesson 1   Breakfast

¡Ven conmigo! and En camino Resources
- *Teaching Transparencies 8-A* and *8-1*
- *Video Program* and *Video Guide*, Chapter 8

Materials you will need
- Index cards, glue, scissors
- Magazines, poster board, markers
- Empty food containers

Language and Culture Objectives
Students will
- learn cultural information about breakfast in Spanish-speaking countries
- learn phrases to talk about breakfast foods

Motivate
- Ask students what they eat for breakfast during the week. On weekends?

Teach
1. *Culture*   Continental-style breakfasts are common in Latin America and Spain. They usually consist of juice, fresh fruit, and bread. Freshly-made juice is often served to accompany meals in many Latin American countries. It is also available from many street vendors and juice stands. Some common juices are made from papayas, pineapples, oranges, and passion fruit. Have students check their local supermarket to see if any of these juices are available. If they are, have a juice tasting.

2. *Visual Learners*   Show students *Teaching Transparency 8-A* to present breakfast food vocabulary. Use *Teaching Transparency 8-1* to have students talk about what the people pictured in the breakfast scene are eating. Play the Chapter 8 videoclips of beverage commercials without sound. Have students guess what type of beverage is being advertised in each.

3. *Language Learning*   Have students make picture flashcards of breakfast vocabulary. Students may draw the breakfast foods and drinks or clip magazine pictures and paste them to one side of an index card. On the other side of the card they write the word in Spanish. For **comer, beber,** and **desayuno,** students can draw someone eating, someone drinking, and a breakfast scene.

4. *Listening*   Have students listen as you read a script of two people talking about what they like to eat and drink for breakfast. As you say the words for breakfast foods, have students hold up the appropriate vocabulary cards. Give students a little time after each sentence to find the correct flashcard. Script: 1. **Me gusta beber leche.**; 2. **¿Te gusta la fruta?**; 3. **Me gusta el cereal.**; 4. **No me gusta para nada el tocino.**; 5. **Me gusta mucho el jugo de naranja.**; 6. **¿Te gusta el pan tostado?**

5. *Speaking*   Give students three minutes to ask as many people as possible what they like for breakfast using **¿Te gusta...?** Then discuss which are the most commonly eaten foods.

6. *Writing*   Have students complete Activity Master 6.1 to practice breakfast vocabulary.

Additional Practice
- *Visual Learners*   Have students use their flashcards to quiz a partner on breakfast vocabulary. One partner holds up the picture side of the card and the other names the breakfast food or drink in Spanish. When they have gone through all the cards once, the partners switch roles.

- *Project*   Have students draw or clip pictures out of magazines to show their typical weekday and weekend breakfasts. Then have them label the pictures. Have students label their posters **Me gusta el desayuno.**

Close
- *Game*   Place empty breakfast food and drink containers, cereal boxes, juice cans, and so on, on a table. Have students match the breakfast food and drink with the correct flashcard. This can also be done with two sets of flashcards on a table.

Activity Master 6.1   Breakfast

1 Match the picture of the breakfast food or drink with the sentence about it in Spanish.

_____ 1. Me gusta beber jugo con el desayuno.   **a**

_____ 2. Me gusta beber leche con el desayuno.   **b**

_____ 3. Me gusta comer pan tostado para el desayuno.   **c**

_____ 4. Para el desayuno me gusta comer fruta.   **d**

_____ 5. Me gusta comer huevos y tocino para el desayuno.   **e**

_____ 6. Para el desayuno me gusta comer cereal.   **f**

2 Find and circle the ten breakfast words that are hidden below. The words appear horizontally and vertically.

cereal
leche
pan dulce
jugo de naranja
huevos
fruta
pan tostado
tocino
plátano

```
L B A P U E S E A C A C E R F I N
U I N A A E C U A M O R Á L U C L
G A C N Í H J S E E I T Ú C O S T
I N U T G L A T E T U A P L Ñ T O
J U G O D E N A R A N J A A O E C
V C C S A C I Ñ L O S A N L N R I
N E I T O H U E V O S P D O X E N
E R D A S E U H O F D U U Y A A O
Z E A D J F R U T A P E L T J L T
U A R O P L Á T A N O R C A Í R U
L L R U G U X A N P Y O E I Q G Y
```

3 Write the foods you like for breakfast in the space below.

Me gusta comer _____

_____ para el desayuno.

UNIT 6 · Food and Beverages   Lesson 2   Lunch

¡Ven conmigo! and En camino Resources
- *Teaching Transparencies 8-B* and *8-1*
- *En camino Annotated Teacher's Edition*
- *Interactive CD-ROM Tutor,* Disc 2

Materials you will need
- Transparency marker
- Colored construction paper, scissors, glue
- Colored markers

Language and Culture Objectives
Students will
- learn when lunch is eaten
- learn phrases to talk about lunch foods

Motivate
- Ask students what they like to eat for lunch. Ask them which lunch foods are common on the cafeteria menu and which lunch foods people usually bring from home.

Teach
1. *Culture* In many Spanish-speaking countries, it is common for families to go home for lunch. Lunch, which is usually served around 2:00 or 3:00 PM, is often the largest meal of the day, and is called **la comida.** It's typically a heavier meal than lunch is in the United States. It often consists of soup, meat, or fish with rice and vegetables, followed by a dessert.

2. *Visual Learners* Display *Teaching Transparency 8-B* to present lunch vocabulary. Say each word and have students repeat after you.

3. *Listening* Talk about which foods you like to eat for lunch. Have students check off the words on their vocabulary list as they hear them. You may also display *Teaching Transparency 8-1* and talk about what the people in the bottom lunch scene are eating. Label the transparency with one letter for each person: *a, b, c,* and *d.* Have students number one to four and write the letter of the person who is eating the food you are describing.

4. *Writing* Have students use Activity Master 6.2 to practice lunch vocabulary.

5. *Project* Have students cut construction paper in fourths to make "lunch trays." Then have them make construction paper replicas of lunch food and drink items that fit within the borders of the "tray." They make six cards, for example, an apple, a bowl of soup, a sandwich . . . They paste or tape each item on its own rectangle "tray." These cards may be used for students to quiz each other on vocabulary or to play Go Fish® as described below.

Additional Practice
- *Visual Learners* Have students use the *Interactive CD-ROM Tutor,* Disc 2, Chapter 8, Activities 2 and 4, to practice recognizing food vocabulary.

- *History Link* Ask students what their favorite foods are. Use the information in the **Enlaces** presentation on pages 112–113 of the *En camino Annotated Teacher's Edition* to tell students if the foods are originally from Europe or the Americas. Call out the names of foods from the list in **Enlaces** and have students guess if they are originally from the Americas or Europe. Make a **Nuevo Mundo** and **Viejo Mundo** list of foods on the board.

Close
- *Game* In groups of four, have students play Go Fish with their construction paper replicas of food items. Students try to find matches for their food items by asking ¿**Tienes...?** Students may also use their flashcards as playing cards, as long as they hide the picture or word.

UNIT 6

Activity Master 6.2   Lunch

1 Write the food items under the appropriate category on the menu below.

manzana

té frío

sándwich de atún

plátano

sándwich de crema de maní

refresco

leche

sopa de pollo

SÁNDWICHES

_____

_____

FRUTAS

_____

_____

SOPA

_____

BEBIDAS

_____

_____

_____

2 Match what each person says they like for lunch with the correct drawing. Write the name of the person in the space provided.

Victoria

Lupe

Sebastián

_____ 1. Me gusta comer pollo y beber té frío.

_____ 2. Me gusta comer sopa y un sándwich y beber leche.

_____ 3. Me gusta comer un sándwich de crema de maní y una manzana.

UNIT 6 · Food and Beverages Lesson 3 Dinner

¡Ven conmigo! and Adelante/En camino Resources
- *Teaching Transparency 8-D*
- *Interactive CD-ROM Tutor,* Disc 2
- *Adelante Annotated Teacher's Edition*

Materials you will need
- Photos of food from magazines
- Construction paper, scissors, glue sticks, and pens, colored pencils or markers
- Drawing paper or poster board

Language and Culture Objectives
Students will
- learn cultural information about dinner
- learn phrases to talk about dinner foods

Motivate
- Ask students what time they usually eat dinner. What are their favorite dinner meals?

Teach
1. *Culture* In many Spanish-speaking countries, the evening meal is often served at 8:00 or 9:00 PM, and is a lighter meal than dinner in the United States. Ask students when they eat the big meal of the day. What are the advantages and disadvantages of eating the main meal earlier in the day?

2. *Visual Learners* Display *Teaching Transparency 8-D* or clip pictures of dinner foods from magazines to present dinner vocabulary. Have students repeat the new vocabulary as you present each word visually and aloud. Ask individual students if they like the food you are presenting. For example, **¿Te gusta comer zanahorias? Sí, me gusta comer zanahorias.**

3. *Tactile Learners* Distribute construction paper, scissors, glue sticks, and pens, colored pencils or markers. Have students make the foods and beverages listed in the **Vocabulario** on page 69 out of construction paper. Tell students to write the Spanish name of each food

on the back of each item. Then have pairs of students use their foods and beverages made of construction paper as flashcards to practice.

4. *Listening* Have students make small PONGA cards, with 9 food or beverage items. See page 19J of *Adelante Annotated Teacher's Edition* for detailed instructions. Talk about dinner food and beverages and have students cover the appropriate items as you mention them. The first student with three items in a row wins.

5. *Writing* Have students complete Activity Master 6.3 to practice dinner vocabulary.

Additional Practice
- *Visual Learners* Have students use the *Interactive CD-ROM Tutor,* Disc 2, Chapter 8, Activity 3 to hear descriptions of food.
- *Project* Have students make posters of their favorite dinner. Have them label the foods and beverages in Spanish. They can label the poster **Mi cena favorita.**

Close
- *Game* Have students work in groups of three. Students 1 and 2 sit facing each other, and Student 3 sits behind Student 2. Student 3 shows a food or beverage made of construction paper to Student 1. Student 1 describes the item in English to Student 2, who guesses the name of the item in Spanish. The group who describes and guesses the most items correctly in one minute wins.

Activity Master 6.3 **Dinner**

1 Look at the picture below to see what food the people in the restaurant are thinking about. Write each person's name under the menu he or she is thinking about.

Manuel   **Marimar**   **Sofía**

Pollo, arroz y frijoles	*Pescado, zanahorias y maíz*	*Bistec, papas fritas y ensalada*

1. _____   2. _____   3. _____

2 Your grandmother would like to cook a special dinner for your birthday. Write the items you would like to eat from the words in the box below.

pollo   pastel   leche   ensalada   té frío

zanahorias   bistec   papas fritas   fruta

Meat: _____

Vegetable: _____

Beverage: _____

Dessert: _____

UNIT 6

UNIT 6 · Food and Beverages   Lesson 4   At the Restaurant

¡Ven conmigo! and *En camino* Resources
- *Teaching Transparencies 8-3* and *8-C*
- *Interactive CD-ROM Tutor,* Disc 2

Materials you will need
- Disposable plates, cups, forks, knives, and spoons
- Magazines that picture restaurants and dishes
- Food items made from construction paper from Lessons 2 and 3

Language and Culture Objectives
Students will
- learn cultural information about restaurants
- learn phrases to order food in restaurants

Motivate
- Ask students how they order food in a restaurant. What phrases do they use? What phrases does the server use?

Teach
1. *Culture* When Spaniards and Latin Americans eat with a fork and knife, they don't switch hands after they cut their food as many people do in the United States. The knife stays in the right hand as the person eats the food from the fork in the left hand. First, model this way of cutting and eating. Then, using plastic forks and knives, have students pretend to use a knife and fork as people do in many parts of Spain and Latin America. Ask them how it feels. Suggest they try the same eating technique at their next meal.

2. *Visual Learners* Display *Teaching Transparency 8-C* to present eating-utensil and table-setting vocabulary. Assign students to groups of four. One student will be the waiter or waitress. The other three are customers. Distribute plastic utensils to the waiter or waitress in each group. One at a time, the customers ask for different items. **¿Me puede traer una cuchara?** The first student in each group to get all three pieces of silverware, wins. Use *Teaching Transparency 8-3* to present restaurant vocabulary such as *waiter* and *waitress.*

3. *Language Learning* Have students make picture flashcards of restaurant vocabulary or distribute plastic tableware for them to label.

4. *Listening* List food and beverage items on the board. Have students write them down. Read the following dialogue. Have students check off the items the customer orders.
   - **Camarero, quisiera la sopa de pollo, pan y una ensalada.**
   - **¿Y para beber, señorita?**
   - **Quisiera leche.**
   - **La sopa de pollo, pan, una ensalada y leche.**
   - **Gracias. ¿Me puede traer una cuchara?**

5. *Writing* Have students complete Activity Master 6.4 to practice phrases used to order food in restaurants.

Additional Practice
- *Visual Learners* Have students use the *Interactive CD-ROM Tutor,* Disc 2, Chapter 8, Activity 6, to practice phrases used to order or serve food.

- *Project* Have students draw or clip pictures of restaurants from magazines. The scene must include at least ten vocabulary items from this unit. Students label the vocabulary in Spanish and label the scene **El Restaurante.**

Close
- *Game* Have students work in small groups. Have one student spread food items made from construction paper from Lessons 2 and 3 on a table and secretly place a coin under one of them. Students win points by ordering as many food items as possible without ordering the item that hides the coin. Each item is worth one point. The student may stop ordering at any time during his or her turn. If the student orders the item with the coin hidden under it, he or she loses the points from that turn. The first student to get 20 points wins.

Activity Master 6.4   **At the Restaurant**

1 Decide whether the following statements would be said by customer or a server. Write **C** in the blank next to the sentence if a **customer** would more be likely to say it and **S** if a **server** would be more likely to say it.

_____ 1. Quisiera té frío.

_____ 2. ¿Me puede traer una cuchara, por favor?

_____ 3. ¿Y para beber?

_____ 4. ¿Qué quiere usted?

_____ 5. Quisiera pollo con arroz.

_____ 6. Buenos días, ¿quiere usted un menú, señorita?

_____ 7. Quisiera un bistec, por favor.

_____ 8. ¿Me puede traer el menú?

2 Write the missing words in the conversation between the server and the customers in the spaces provided below. Remember to capitalize words at the beginning of sentences. One word will be used twice.

quiere	quisiera	qué	me puede	beber

1.   **CAMARERO**   ¿_____ quiere usted, señora?

2. **SEÑORA VILLANUEVA**   _____ el pollo, las zanahorias y el arroz.

3.   **CAMARERO**   ¿Y para _____, señora?

4. **SEÑORA VILLANUEVA**   _____ el té frío.

5.   **CAMARERO**   ¿Qué _____ usted, señor?

6.   **SEÑOR VILLANUEVA**   Quisiera el bistec, las papas fritas y un refresco.

                                          Y, ¿_____ traer una servilleta?

UNIT 6 · Food and Beverages   Vocabulary

LESSON 1 · Breakfast

beber *to drink*	**el jugo de naranja** *orange juice*
el cereal *cereal*	**la leche** *milk*
comer *to eat*	**el pan dulce** *sweet roll*
el desayuno *breakfast*	**el pan tostado** *toast*
la fruta *fruit*	**el plátano** *banana*
los huevos *eggs*	**el tocino** *bacon*

LESSON 2 · Lunch

el almuerzo *lunch*	**el pollo** *chicken*
el atún *tuna*	**la sopa** *soup*
la crema de maní *peanut butter*	**el refresco** *soft drink*
el jamón *ham*	**el té frío** *iced tea*
la manzana *apple*	**el sándwich** *sandwich*
la pizza *pizza*	**el vaso de leche** *glass of milk*

LESSON 3 · Dinner

el arroz *rice*	**las papas fritas** *French fries*
el bistec *steak*	**el pastel** *cake*
la cena *dinner*	**el pescado** *fish*
la ensalada *salad*	**el postre** *dessert*
los frijoles *beans*	**la zanahoria** *carrot*
el maíz *corn*	

LESSON 4 · At the Restaurant

¿Me puede traer...? *Can you bring me . . .?*	**la cuchara** *spoon*
¿Qué quiere usted? *What would you like?*	**el cuchillo** *knife*
¿Y para beber? *And to drink?*	**el menú** *menu*
¿Y para comer? *And to eat?*	**el plato** *plate*
Quisiera... *I would like . . .*	**la servilleta** *napkin*
la camarera *waitress*	**el tenedor** *fork*
el camarero *waiter*	

U N I T 6

UNIT 6 · Food and Beverages   Review and Assessment

¡Ven conmigo! and Adelante Resources
- *Interactive CD-ROM Tutor,* Disc 2

Materials you will need
- Unit 6 vocabulary flashcards
- Drawing paper

Language and Culture Assessment Objectives

Students will

- show their knowledge of breakfast, lunch, dinner, and restaurant vocabulary in Spanish
- show their knowledge of food customs in the Spanish-speaking world
- express their knowledge orally and in the form of an in-class project

Review

1. Call out a breakfast food and have students hold up the correct flashcard.
2. Call out a lunch food and have students hold up the correct flashcard.
3. Have students ask and answer **¿Te gusta comer cereal?** in pairs.
4. Have students ask and tell each other **¿Te gustaría comer un sándwich?** in pairs.

Assessment Options

Written

- Have students complete **¡Ya lo sé!**, Unit 6. You will find the script for the listening activity on page 115 of this guide.
- *Project* Have students make restaurant menus in Spanish that include breakfast, lunch, and dinner items. Students title the sections of the menus **el desayuno, el almuerzo, la cena, las bebidas,** and **los**

postres. Under each of the three meals, they write two complete selections. For example, for breakfast the two items could be: **huevos, tocino y pan tostado** and **cereal, leche y un plátano.** They write two individual items under **bebidas** and **postres.** Students may choose the name of their restaurant. Suggest that they use the format **"El Restaurante de Juan"** if they want to name it Juan's Restaurant.

Oral

1. Ask the student **¿Te gusta comer... para el desayuno?**
2. Place five food flashcards on the desk for the student to identify.
3. Ask the student **¿Te gusta beber... para el almuerzo?**
4. Ask the student **¿Te gusta comer... para la cena?**
5. Ask the student when the main meal of the day is in many Spanish-speaking countries. (at 2:00 or 3:00 PM)

CD-ROM

- Have students use the *Interactive CD-ROM Tutor,* Disc 2, Chapter 8, Activities 2, 4, and 6, to practice food vocabulary.

UNIT 6

UNIT 6 · Food and Beverages   ¡Ya lo sé!   Total Points: 40

A. Breakfast

Listen as Luisa and Roberto talk about what they like to eat for breakfast. As they say what they like, place a check mark in the box under the appropriate name. Only five of the items they mention are listed here. (10 points)

	Luisa	Roberto
1. leche		
2. huevos		
3. jugo de naranja		
4. pan tostado		
5. tocino		

SCORE [____]

B. Lunch

It's almost lunch time and people are thinking of what they like to eat. Match the sentence about what the person likes to have for lunch with the picture of the person thinking about it. Write the letter of the picture in the blank. (12 points)

a. Victoria   b. Lupe   c. Sebastián

_____ 1. Me gusta beber leche y comer un sándwich de atún y sopa de pollo.

_____ 2. Me gusta comer un sándwich de crema de maní y una manzana.

_____ 3. Me gusta beber té frío. Me gusta comer pollo, arroz y legumbres.

SCORE [____]

UNIT 6

UNIT 6 · Food and Beverages   **¡Ya lo sé!**   *continued*

C. Dinner at the Restaurant

Match the customer's statements and requests with the correct pictures. One picture is *not* used. (14 points)

_____ 1. ¿Me puede traer un tenedor?

_____ 2. ¿Me puede traer una servilleta?

_____ 3. Quisiera el pescado.

_____ 4. Quisiera el jamón con piña.

_____ 5. Quisiera fruta, por favor.

_____ 6. Quisiera leche, por favor.

_____ 7. Quisiera una ensalada con zanahorias.

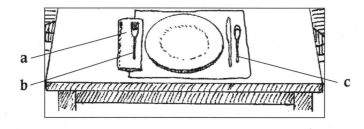

a
b
c

d

e

f

g

h

SCORE [ ]

D. La comida

Based on what you've learned about meals in Spanish-speaking countries, write **c** for **cierto** or **f** for **falso** in the space provided. (4 points)

_____ 1. Dinner is usually a light meal late in the evening.

_____ 2. Lunch is usually around 11:30.

SCORE [ ]

TOTAL SCORE [/40]

UNIT 7 · Around Town　　　Lesson 1　　　Places

¡Ven conmigo! and Adelante/En camino Resources
- *Teaching Transparency 4-2*
- *Video Program* and *Video Guide*, Chapter 4

Materials you will need
- Index cards
- Travel magazines, scissors
- Drawing paper, pens, tape
- Name tags

Language and Culture Objectives

Students will
- learn about Mexican murals
- learn phrases to talk about where they are going

Motivate
- Ask students what their favorite place or building in town is and why.

Teach
1. *Culture*　Ask students if they know what a mural is. (a large picture painted on a wall or ceiling) Have they ever seen one? Where? There are many murals in Mexico City. Famous Mexican artists, such as Diego Rivera, José Clemente Orozco, and David Siqueiros painted them to beautify the city and to teach Mexico's history through art.

2. *Visual Learners*　Display *Teaching Transparency 4-2* to present city vocabulary. Show students Chapter 4 **De antemano** video footage of a store, restaurant, house, post office, and library. You may wish to play the videotape without sound. Say the names of the buildings on the transparency in Spanish and have students repeat after you. (**tienda, restaurante, casa, correo, biblioteca**) Teach students to ask and answer this question: **¿Adónde vas? Voy a la.../Voy al...** (**al** is **a** + **el**)

3. *Listening*　On the board create a word box of city vocabulary or display *Teaching Transparency 4-2*. Have students number one to four on a piece of paper. Tell students four places you will be going in the city. Say sentences in Spanish about where you will go, for example, **Voy al correo.** Have students write the word **correo** for number one.

4. *Language Learning*　Have students make flashcards with pictures of buildings they clip from travel magazines. Students paste or tape the pictures to one side of an index card and write the word in Spanish on the other side. Then, have the students work in pairs, quizzing each other on city vocabulary.

5. *Speaking*　Have students work in pairs with the flashcards for city vocabulary. Partner A asks Partner B **¿Adónde vas?** and shows a picture vocabulary card. Partner B responds **Voy a la.../Voy al...** and names the building in the picture. Then the partners switch roles.

6. *Writing*　Have students complete Activity Master 7.1 to practice city vocabulary and phrases to ask and tell where people are going.

Additional Practice
- *Project*　Have students draw a map of a city that includes all the vocabulary from this lesson. Students draw or clip pictures from magazines and label the city buildings. Ask students to postpone naming the streets until Lesson 2. Suggest that students leave the edges of their city drawing open for further "city development" in the next two lessons. These posters may be used as a game board in Lesson 2 (see page 75).

Close
- *Game*　Give each student a name tag with a city vocabulary word on it written in Spanish. The name tags go on their backs, so they cannot see their vocabulary word. Then students circulate around the room giving each other clues in English about the place names on their backs.

Activity Master 7.1

Places

1 Look over the list of Saturday errands listed below that you and your older sister plan to do. From the Spanish word box, choose the place where you can do your errand. Complete the sentence with the place you will go.

MODELO   Babysit younger brother   **Voy a casa.**

1) Return books	
2) Go swimming	
3) Buy a snack	
4) Mail letter to pen pal	
5) Go to a movie	

al correo	al cine
a la tienda	a casa
a la biblioteca	a la piscina
al supermercado	

1. Voy _____

2. Voy _____

3. Voy _____

4. Voy _____

5. Voy _____

2 Complete the crossword puzzle in Spanish according to the picture clues.

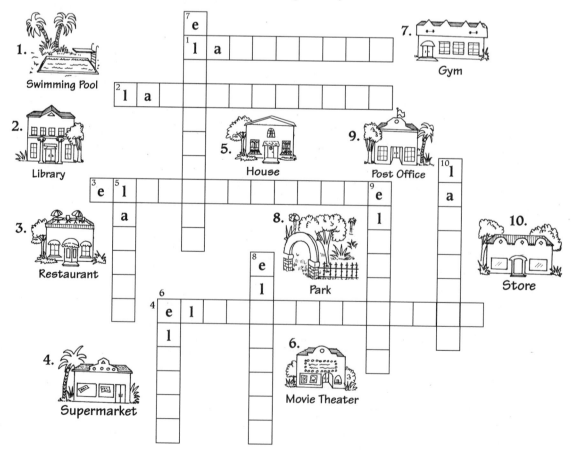

Unit 7 · Around Town   Lesson 2   Directions

¡Ven conmigo! and Adelante Resources
- *Teaching Transparency 4-2*

Materials you will need
- Transparency marker
- Paper signs labeled with street names, tape
- City vocabulary cards from Unit 7, Lesson 1
- City maps from Unit 7, Lesson 1 Project

Language and Culture Objectives
Students will
- learn cultural information about street names in Latin America
- learn phrases to give and understand directions

Motivate
- Ask students where the nearest gas station, convenience store, or some other building near school is. Tell students they will learn to give and receive simple directions in Spanish in this lesson.

Teach
1. *Culture* In Latin American countries, streets often are named for important dates in the country's history and also for famous people. For example, a street in Mexico City is named for the date the Mexican revolution began in 1910, **20 de Noviembre.** In Quito, Ecuador, there is an avenue named for their Independence Day, **Avenida 24 de Mayo.** In Buenos Aires, Argentina, the **Avenida 9 de Julio** is named for their Independence Day.

2. *Visual Learners* Display *Teaching Transparency 4-2* to introduce these words and phrases: **la calle, la avenida, ¿Dónde está...?,** and **Está en...** Mark street names on the transparency using **calle** and **avenida.** See the Project below for street name suggestions. Then ask **¿Dónde está la biblioteca?** Say the directions, for example, **Está en la Calle Ocho y la Avenida de la Gran Cultura.** Have students repeat after you and practice giving directions with you.

3. *Kinesthetic Learners* Have students imagine that the classroom is a city and each desk is one city block. Students use their Unit 7, Lesson 1, city vocabulary cards and choose a store or other building. Have them put the card on their desk as a sign for their building. Post paper signs to give the aisles names like **La Calle San Juan, El Camino Real,** or **La Avenida Central.** Have one student ask, in Spanish, where a particular building is located: **¿Dónde está la tienda?** Tell the student where the building is, for example, **Está en la Calle San Juan y la Avenida Central.** When the student arrives at his or her destination, he or she answers another student's question about where a particular building is, and so on, until all the locations in the "city" have been found.

4. *Writing* Have students complete Activity Master 7.2 to practice writing and responding to directions.

Additional Practice
- *Project* Have students label the streets of their city maps from Unit 7, Lesson 1, in Spanish with names using **calle** or **avenida.** Suggest that students write street names that represent names of countries, important dates, or famous people, for example, **Calle Colombia** or **Avenida 4 de Julio.**

Close
- *Game* Have students use their city maps from Unit 7, Lesson 1. Two partners use one of their two maps as a game board. They place a scrap of paper that represents a dollar bill on each location. Then, one partner asks **¿Dónde está el cine?,** for example. His or her partner responds **Está en la Avenida 4 de Julio y la Calle Pablo Picasso.** The partner who gives successful directions wins the scrap paper at the destination. They take turns giving directions until they have collected all of the scraps. The partner with the most "money," wins.

Activity Master 7.2   Directions

UNIT 7

1 Follow directions to find your way around this new city. Match the directions with the building it describes. Write the letter in the blank next to the directions.

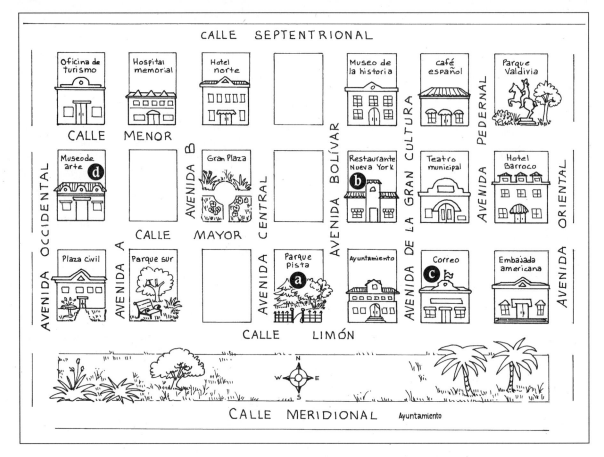

_____ 1. Está en la Calle Mayor y la Avenida Occidental.

_____ 2. Está en la Calle Limón y la Avenida Central.

_____ 3. Está en la Calle Mayor y la Avenida Bolívar.

_____ 4. Está en la Calle Limón y la Avenida de la Gran Cultura.

2 You are on vacation in another city with your family. You and your family want to do the following activities. Match each item with the appropriate building on the map above. Write the name of the building in the space below.

1. rollerblade in a safe area _____

2. see some of Picasso's paintings _____

3. mail postcards _____

4. eat pizza _____

Unit 7 · Around Town   Lesson 3   More Places to See

¡Ven conmigo! and En camino Resources
- *Teaching Transparency 7-A*
- *Interactive CD-ROM Tutor,* Disc 2

Materials you will need
- Index cards
- City maps from Lessons 1 and 2
- Rulers, scissors, markers or colored pencils

Language and Culture Objectives
Students will
- learn about a museum of anthropology in Mexico
- learn phrases to talk about places for free-time activities

Motivate
- Ask students what places they would recommend to a visitor in their town. What would be the five most interesting places? Would students recommend a particular park, a museum, a historical building, the zoo?

Teach
1. *Culture*   In the region where Mexico is today, great civilizations flourished thousands of years before the Spanish arrived. The Olmec, Toltec, Maya, Aztec, and other civilizations created sculpture, jewelry, ceramics, and other artifacts that are preserved at the National Museum of Anthropology in Mexico City. The museum has exhibits showing the last 8000 years of history of the region's people, architecture, and art. If possible, display books, encyclopedias, or Web sites that contain examples of Maya or Aztec art.

2. *Visual Learners*   Display *Teaching Transparency 7-A* to introduce additional places around town. Say the words as you point out the vocabulary on the transparency. Have students repeat the new vocabulary after you. Present the question ¿**Te gustaría ir...?** using the names of the places in this lesson. For example, ¿**Te gustaría ir al acuario?** Then model the answer **Sí, me gustaría ir al acuario** and have students repeat the phrases after you.

3. *Language Learning*   Have students make picture flashcards of this lesson's vocabulary. Distribute copies of *Transparency Master 7-A.* Students may draw the vocabulary or clip art from their copy of the transparency and attach it to index cards. Then they write the Spanish vocabulary on the other side. Have partners use their flashcards to practice the vocabulary.

4. *Speaking*   Have students work in pairs. Ask the partners to invite each other to three or four places using vocabulary from this lesson. Make sure to list the new vocabulary on the board or give students copies of the vocabulary lists.

5. *Writing*   Have students complete Activity Master 7.3 to practice vocabulary for places where free-time activities occur.

Additional Practice
- *Visual Learners*   Have students use the *Interactive CD-ROM Tutor,* Disc 2, Chapter 7, Activity 1, to practice vocabulary for free-time activities. (Students may need a hint that **boda** means *wedding* and **cumpleaños** means *birthday.*)

- *Project*   Have students continue working on their city maps that they began in Lessons 1 and 2. Have them add buildings such as a museum, aquarium, and other places representing vocabulary from this lesson.

Close
- *Game*   Divide the class into two teams and have students play **Dibújalo.** Suggest that students draw things that would be found at the places in this lesson's vocabulary. For example, fish and other marine life would be found at an aquarium, acrobats and clowns at a circus, and so on.

Activity Master 7.3   **More Places to See**

UNIT 7

1 Match the following pictures with the statements that describe them. One answer will not be used.

_____ 1.    _____ 3.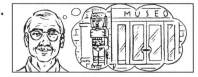

_____ 2.    _____ 4.

a. Me gustaría ir a un parque de atracciones con mi amigo.

b. Me gustaría ir al museo de antropología el sábado.

c. Me gustaría ir al circo.

d. Me gustaría ir al acuario.

e. Me gustaría ir al zoológico con mi familia.

2 If you were in an anthropology museum, you might see the following design. To see an animal often found in Maya weaving, color the numbered squares. Use the color key below.

1 = **rojo**   2 = **verde**   3 = **amarillo**   4 = **anaranjado**

4	1	1	1	1	1	1	1	1	1	1	1	1	1	1	1	1	4
1	4	1	1	1	1	1	1	1	1	1	2	1	1	1	1	4	1
4	1	1	1	1	1	1	1	1	1	2	2	2	1	1	1	1	4
1	4	1	1	1	2	2	1	1	2	2	1	2	2	2	1	4	1
4	1	1	1	2	2	2	2	1	3	2	1	2	2	2	1	1	4
1	4	1	2	2	1	2	2	1	1	2	2	1	2	2	1	4	1
4	1	1	2	1	1	3	2	2	1	3	2	2	1	2	1	1	4
1	4	1	2	2	1	1	3	2	2	1	2	2	1	1	1	4	1
4	1	1	3	2	2	1	1	3	2	2	2	1	1	1	1	1	4
1	4	1	1	3	2	2	1	1	1	2	1	1	1	1	1	4	1
4	1	1	1	1	3	2	2	1	1	1	1	1	1	1	1	1	4
1	4	1	1	1	1	3	2	2	1	1	1	1	1	1	1	4	1

Unit 7 · Around Town   Lesson 4   Zoo Animals

¡Ven conmigo! and En camino Resources
- *Video Program* and *Video Guide,* Chapter 12
- *En camino* Annotated Teacher's Edition

Materials you will need
- Nature magazines with photos of animals
- Index cards, scissors, tape or glue
- Large sheets of paper
- Markers, colored pencils, or paint

Language and Culture Objectives
Students will
- learn about wildlife preserves in Latin America
- learn vocabulary for animals found in zoos

Motivate
- Ask students to talk about their favorite wild animals. Have they seen the animal on television, at a zoo, or in person? What is unique about the animal? What part of the world does the animal come from?

Teach
1. *Culture* Tell students about some of the extensive parks and wildlife preserves found in Latin America. Some examples are El Yunque, a rainforest in Puerto Rico, the Galápagos Islands off the coast of Ecuador, and Manuel Antonio National Park in Costa Rica. These parks preserve unique wildlife: the coquí frog in Puerto Rico, the Galápagos tortoise and marine iguana in the Galápagos Islands, and the squirrel monkey in Costa Rica. Play **De antemano, A continuación** in the *¡Ven conmigo!* or *En camino* video for Chapter 12 to show footage of El Yunque, also known as the Caribbean National Forest.

2. *Visual Learners* Show students pictures you have clipped from wildlife magazines to introduce vocabulary for zoo animals found on the **Vocabulario** page. Say the word in Spanish as you show the picture of the animal and have students repeat after you.

3. *Language Learning* Have students use copies of *National Geographic®* or other nature magazines to make picture flashcards. Students write the word in Spanish on one side and attach a picture to the other side of an index card. In pairs, have students practice vocabulary for zoo animals using their new flashcards.

4. *Music Link* Teach students to sing *El señor Pérez tiene un zoo* to the tune of *Old MacDonald Had a Farm.* Write the words on the board or on a transparency. "**El señor Pérez tiene un zoo, ¡Ay, el ruido, ay! En su zoo tiene (una serpiente), ¡Ay, el ruido, ay! Con un (noise of snake) aquí, y un (noise of snake) allí, por todos lados** (noise of snake three times). **El señor Pérez tiene un zoo, ¡Ay, el ruido, ay!**" Continue, replacing the animal in parentheses with one of the following animals: **un elefante, un león, un loro, un mono.**

5. *Writing* Have students complete Activity Master 7.4 to practice writing and recognizing vocabulary for animals often found in zoos.

Additional Practice
- *Culture* Present the information from **Enlaces** on pages 72–73 of *En camino,* which contains information on several of the unique animals of the Galápagos Islands.

- *Project* Tell students to imagine they have been asked to paint or draw murals for the walls of a zoo. What animals would they paint? Have students work in pairs to decide which animal from the vocabulary in this lesson they would like to illustrate or paint. They label the animal in Spanish. Then have the class paste their animals on a large piece of butcher paper, which can be used as class decoration.

Close
- *Game* Have students play charades to practice vocabulary for zoo animals.

Activity Master 7.4   **Zoo Animals**

UNIT 7

1 Unscramble the following words to find the names of ten animals often found in zoos.

1. L R C O D O C O I   _____

2. O M N O   _____

3. R O G A T U T   _____

4. O R L O   _____

5. R E S E N I T E P   _____

6. G R T I E   _____

7. E R A C B   _____

8. E Ó L N   _____

9. L E F E N A T E   _____

10. S O O   _____

2 The Galápagos Islands are in the Pacific Ocean, off the west coast of Ecuador, South America. Many of the islands are part of an Ecuadorean national park created to protect the unique animals that live there. Read the information about the Galápagos tortoise and answer the questions below.

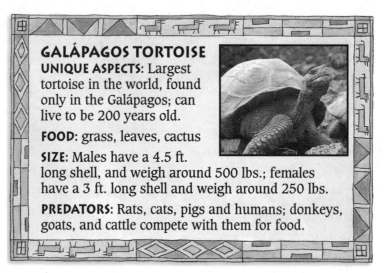

GALÁPAGOS TORTOISE
UNIQUE ASPECTS: Largest tortoise in the world, found only in the Galápagos; can live to be 200 years old.
FOOD: grass, leaves, cactus
SIZE: Males have a 4.5 ft. long shell, and weigh around 500 lbs.; females have a 3 ft. long shell and weigh around 250 lbs.
PREDATORS: Rats, cats, pigs and humans; donkeys, goats, and cattle compete with them for food.

1. If a Galápagos tortoise celebrated its 100th birthday today, what year was it born?

_____

2. What does a Galápagos tortoise eat?

_____

_____

3. What are three things the Galápagos tortoise needs to be protected from?

_____

_____

Unit 7 · Around Town   Vocabulary

LESSON 1 · Places

¿Adónde vas? *Where are you going?*

Voy al/a la... *I am going to the . . .*

al (a + el) *to the*

la biblioteca *library*

la casa *house, home*

el cine *movie theater*

el correo *post office*

el gimnasio *gym*

el parque *park*

la piscina *swimming pool*

el restaurante *restaurante*

el supermercado *supermarket*

la tienda *store*

LESSON 2 · Directions

la avenida *avenue*

la calle *street*

¿Dónde está...? *Where is . . .?*

Está en... *It is on . . .*

y *and*

LESSON 3 · More Places to See

¿Te gustaría ir al.../a la...? *Would you like
to go to the . . .?*

Sí, me gustaría ir al.../a la... *Yes, I would
like to go to the . . .*

el acuario *aquarium*

el campo *country*

el circo *circus*

la ciudad *city*

el lago *lake*

el museo de antropología *anthropology
museum*

el parque de atracciones *amusement park*

el teatro *theater*

el zoológico *zoo*

LESSON 4 · Zoo Animals

la cebra *zebra*

el cocodrilo *crocodile*

el elefante *elephant*

el león *lion*

el loro *parrot*

el mono *monkey*

el oso *bear*

la serpiente *snake*

el tigre *tiger*

la tortuga *tortoise, turtle*

Teacher's Name _____ Class _____ Date _____

 UNIT 7 · Around Town　　　　　　　**Review and Assessment**

¡Ven conmigo! and *Adelante/En camino* Resources
- *Adelante Annotated Teacher's Edition*
- *Interactive CD-ROM Tutor,* Disc 2

Materials you will need
- Vocabulary flashcards for city and animals
- Drawing paper
- Markers or colored pencils
- Copy of Activity Master 7.2

Language and Culture Assessment Objectives

Students will
- show their knowledge of city vocabulary in Spanish
- show their knowledge of culture in the Spanish-speaking world
- express their knowledge orally and in the form of an in-class project

Review
1. Have students hold up the correct flashcard as you call out vocabulary for animals.
2. Call out city vocabulary and have students hold up the correct flashcard.
3. In pairs, have students ask and answer **¿Adónde vas?**
4. In pairs, have students ask and give directions to local stores: **¿Dónde está...?**
5. Have students ask a partner questions such as **¿Te gustaría ir al parque de atracciones?**

Assessment Options
Written
- Have students complete **¡Ya lo sé!**, Unit 7. You will find the script for the listening activity on page 115 of this guide.
- *Project* Have students work in groups of four or five to talk about their idea of an ideal city. Each group decides what five buildings

or places are most important in an ideal city. As each group reports to the class, write the buildings and places they chose on the board. Then have students work in pairs to build a model of one of the structures or places with construction paper and label it in Spanish. When they are finished, lead a class discussion about how the class thinks the city should be organized. Have them work together to combine what they have built into a city model and title it **Nuestra ciudad ideal**. See *Adelante Annotated Teacher's Edition,* Chapter 4, page 141H, for a detailed description of the project.

Oral
1. Show the student a copy of Activity Master 7.2 and ask directions to a particular building: **¿Dónde está...?**
2. Place five picture flashcards of city vocabulary on the desk for the student to identify.
3. Ask the student **¿Adónde vas?** and show the student a picture flashcard of a city building.
4. Ask the student **¿Te gustaría ir al acuario?**
5. Ask the student to say the name of a zoo animal in Spanish.
6. Ask the student what street names in Latin America are often named after. (an important date or other historical events)

CD-ROM
- Have students use the *Interactive CD-ROM Tutor,* Disc 2, Chapter 7, Activity 1, to review places for free-time activities.

Unit 7 · Around Town   **¡Ya lo sé!**   **Total Points: 40**

UNIT 7

A. Where are you going?

Listen as Jorge and Georgina talk about their plans. Match their names to the places they talk about going. (8 points)

ⓐ   ⓑ   ⓒ   ⓓ

1. Georgina   _____   _____

2. Jorge   _____   _____

SCORE [   ]

B. Animals

Match the drawing of the animal with its name in Spanish. (12 points)

_____ **1.** la tortuga   _____ **3.** el loro   _____ **5.** el tigre

_____ **2.** el mono   _____ **4.** la serpiente   _____ **6.** el cocodrilo

SCORE [   ]

Unit 7 · Around Town   ¡Ya lo sé!   *continued*

UNIT 7

C. Directions

Match the directions with the building it describes. Write the letter in the blank next to the directions. Use each letter only once. (12 points)

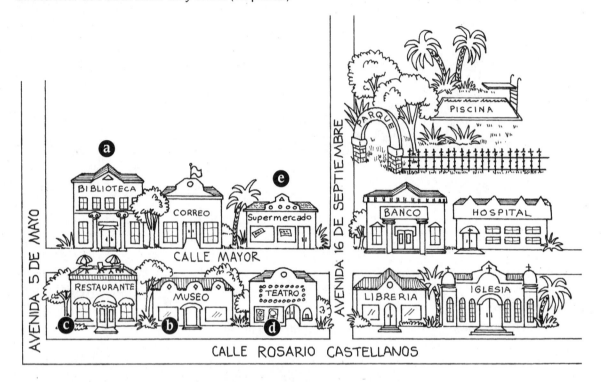

_____ 1. Está en la Calle Mayor y la Avenida 16 de Septiembre.

_____ 2. Está en la Calle Rosario Castellanos y la Avenida 16 de Septiembre.

_____ 3. Está en la Calle Rosario Castellanos y la Avenida 5 de Mayo.

_____ 4. Está en la Calle Mayor y la Avenida 5 de Mayo.   SCORE ☐

D. Los Parques Nacionales

Answer the following questions about national parks in Latin America. (8 points)

1. Which of the following endangered animals are protected in national parks in Latin America? Circle the letters of the two animals that are protected.

   a. elephant   c. squirrel monkey   e. marine iguana

   b. bald eagle   d. blue whale

2. Circle the country which has a national park that protects the animals of Galápagos Islands.

   a. El Salvador   b. Ecuador   c. Argentina

SCORE ☐

TOTAL SCORE ☐ /40

UNIT 8 · Family and Pets Lesson 1 Family Members

¡Ven conmigo! and Adelante Resources
- *Teaching Transparencies 6-A* and *6-1*
- *Video Program* and *Video Guide,* Chapter 6
- *Interactive CD-ROM Tutor,* Disc 2
- *Adelante* Annotated Teacher's Edition

Materials you will need
- Copies of *Teaching Transparency 6-1*
- Drawing paper
- Magazines or newspapers
- Pictures of people
- Tape or glue, scissors

Language and Culture Objectives
Students will
- learn cultural information about families in Spanish-speaking countries
- learn phrases to talk about family members

Motivate
- Ask students to think of the event that brought the largest number of their extended family together. Make a list of the events students suggest (family reunions, birthdays, weddings, funerals, and graduations). Talk about why families make an extra effort to attend certain events.

Teach
1. *Culture* In Spanish-speaking countries it is not uncommon for three generations of a family to live in the same house. Family often includes aunts, uncles, cousins, grandparents, and godparents. The extended family can include members who are not biological relatives, for example, a stepmother (**madrastra**), a stepfather (**padrastro**), stepsister (**hermanastra**), stepbrother (**hermanastro**), half brother (**medio hermano**) or a half sister (**media hermana**). Ask students what their definition of family would be.
2. *Visual Learners* Display *Teaching Transparency 6-A* to introduce vocabulary for family members. Have students repeat after you as you point to the family members in the transparency and say the new vocabulary aloud. Display *Teaching Transparency 6-1* to familiarize students with family trees.
3. *Kinesthetic Learners* Clap the syllables and stress for each vocabulary word, with students repeating after you. Point out the

stress on the words **mamá** and **papá**. Have students take turns clapping a word, and see who can guess which word they are clapping, for example, **mamá** or **hijo**.
4. *Listening* Play the Chapter 6 video dramatic episode. As Raquel talks about her family, have students listen for new vocabulary and check off the members of the family on their copy of the vocabulary sheet from page 93 of this guide.
5. *Writing* Have students complete Activity Master 8.1 to practice vocabulary for family members.

Additional Practice
- *Visual Learners* Have students use the *Interactive CD-ROM Tutor,* Disc 2, Chapter 6, Activity 1, to practice vocabulary for family members.
- *Culture* Present the cultural information about extended family and last names from **Enlaces**, pages 252–253 of *Adelante Annotated Teacher's Edition.*
- *Project* Have each student create a fictitious family tree in which all the vocabulary words for this lesson are used. Students should include themselves in the family tree. Have students create their diagrams. Next, they draw the family members, or cut and paste pictures from magazines. Have students label each family member with their name and family relationship. Save the family trees for use in the next three lessons.

Close
- *Game* Have students play **Dibújalo** to practice vocabulary for family members. Remind students that sketching a family tree can be useful to show which family member it is.

Activity Master 8.1   Family Members

1   Use the family tree below to complete the following sentences. Write the family relationship of the people in the blanks provided.

la hermana

     la hija

el abuelo

    la madre

el padre

1. Juana es _____ de Mario y Luisa.

2. José es _____ de Julia.

3. Julia es _____ de Pedro y Elena.

4. Diana es _____ de Pedro.

5. Mario es _____ de Pedro, Elena y Julia.

2   Sort the family members in the word box by gender. Write the male family members under the column labeled **MASCULINO** and the female family members under the column labeled **FEMENINO**.

hija	hermana	hermano	hijo	padre	madre	abuelo	abuela

MASCULINO   **FEMENINO**

_____   _____

_____   _____

_____   _____

_____   _____

UNIT 8

Unit 8 · Family and Pets   Lesson 2   Introductions

¡Ven conmigo! and Adelante Resources
- *Teaching Transparencies 6-1* and *1-2*
- *Video Program* and *Video Guide*, Ch. 2, 6
- *Adelante Video Program*, Chapter 2

Materials you will need
- Paper and pens
- Foam ball

Language and Culture Objectives
Students will
- learn how Spanish-speakers greet friends
- learn phrases to introduce people

Motivate
- Ask students to imagine that their family (or an imaginary family) is going on a TV talk show, and that each student has to write the introduction for their family. On which TV show would they like their family to appear? How would they introduce their family?

Teach
1. *Culture* Explain how Spanish-speakers often greet one another with a handshake or kiss. In Spain, friends greet each other with a light kiss on both cheeks. Latin Americans kiss on only one cheek. When men greet each other, they often shake hands, pat each other on the back, or hug. Young people often shake hands when they meet or say goodbye. Family members usually greet each other with a kiss. Ask students how they greet their friends and family members. Show **Encuentro cultural** from Chapter 2 of the *Adelante Video Program* about greetings.

2. *Visual Learners* Display *Teaching Transparency 6-1*. Teach students to introduce the people in the family tree as if they were members of their own family: **Éste es mi papá. Ésta es mi hermana.**

3. *Listening* Display *Teaching Transparency 1-2* to teach more vocabulary for introducing people. Introduce the people in the transparency to the class. Teach students to respond to introductions with **Mucho gusto** and **Igualmente.** Have them practice these phrases as a class as you make introductions.

4. *Kinesthetic Learners* Have students work in groups of four or five. Each group stands in a circle. One student at a time introduces the person on his or her left to the person to his or her right using **Ésta es** (name) or **Éste es** (name). The student to the left says **Mucho gusto** and the student to the right says **Igualmente,** and they shake hands. The student who said **Igualmente** continues by introducing the people to either side. Demonstrate this by standing in one of the groups and modeling the introductions, then have students work in their groups until everyone has had a chance to introduce a classmate and to be introduced.

5. *Writing* Have students complete Activity Master 8.2 to practice vocabulary for introductions.

Additional Practice
- *Culture* Tell students that Spanish-speakers will most often say **Bueno** or **Diga,** not **Hola,** when they answer the phone.

- *Project* Have students work in groups to write a script in which fictitious family members are introduced on a TV talk show or game show. They may use their vocabulary lists. Groups script the introductions, such as **Ésta es mi madre, se llama Sara.** Each student chooses to be a family member, a talk show host, or an emcee. Have each group present their show to the class.

Close
- *Game* Have students stand in a circle. Toss a foam ball to a student. This student introduces the person to his or her left to the group. The student who is introduced sits down. The introducer then throws the foam ball to someone else. The game ends when only one person is left.

Activity Master 8.2   Introductions

1 The first day of school is over and Rigoberta and Samuel are meeting for the first time. Use the words in the box to write the missing words from their conversation. Make sure to capitalize the first letter of the word if it begins the sentence.

SAMUEL   Hola, me llamo Samuel.

RIGOBERTA   Hola, Samuel.

SAMUEL   ¿Cómo 1. _____?

RIGOBERTA   2. _____ Rigoberta.

SAMUEL   3. _____, Rigoberta.

RIGOBERTA   4. _____. Hasta mañana.

SAMUEL   Adiós.

igualmente te llamas

me llamo mucho gusto

2 Write the letter of the response to each statement or question below in the space provided. A response may be used more than once.

If someone said . . .

_____ 1. Ésta es mi hermana.

_____ 2. Mucho gusto.

_____ 3. ¿Cómo te llamas?

_____ 4. Éste es mi padre.

A logical response would be . . .

a. Igualmente.

b. Mucho gusto.

c. Me llamo Carlos.

3 Match the family member with Raquel's introductions. In the space provided, write the letter of the person being introduced.

la familia Canales

Me llamo Raquel.

_____ 1. Éste es mi hermano.

_____ 2. Ésta es mi hermana.

_____ 3. Ésta es mi mamá.

_____ 4. Éste es mi papá.

UNIT 8

Unit 8 · Family and Pets | Lesson 3 | Descriptions

¡Ven conmigo! and Adelante Resources

- *Teaching Transparency 3-B*
- *Interactive CD-ROM Tutor,* Disc 2

Materials you will need

- Index cards, scissors, tape or glue
- Magazines
- Drawing paper, markers or colored pencils

Language and Culture Objectives

Students will

- learn affectionate terms for people in Spanish
- learn phrases to describe people

Motivate

- Start describing a TV or movie star and see if students can guess who you are describing. Ask students when it is important to describe someone. (when someone gets lost, to describe a new classmate)

Teach

1. *Culture* Many Spanish-speakers call their grandparents **abuelita** and **abuelito,** which are similar to *grandma* and *grandpa.* Similarly, a good friend might affectionately call Rosa, Rosita and Juan, Juanito. Ask volunteers about nicknames they have.

2. *Visual Learners* Display *Teaching Transparency 3-B* to introduce descriptive words. Point to the people in the picture and say the adjectives aloud. Have students repeat words and phrases after you. For example, **Luis es rubio y simpático.** Explain that descriptive words in Spanish match the gender of the person being described. In the sentence above, Luis is male, so the words describing him end in **-o.** For a girl, the description would be **Teresa es rubia y simpática.** Since Teresa is female, the words describing her end in **-a.** (**Interesante** and **inteligente** are exceptions; they do not change according to gender.) Show examples on the transparency.

3. *Language Learning* Have students make picture flashcards, using magazine clippings that represent the descriptive vocabulary. Students attach the picture to an index card and write the word in Spanish on the other side. Have students practice in pairs, using their flashcards. One partner shows the picture image and the other describes the person in the picture. For example, to describe a tall basketball player they would say **Es alto.**

4. *Writing* Have students complete Activity Master 8.3 to practice describing people.

Additional Practice

- *Visual Learners* Have students use the family tree art in the *Interactive CD-ROM Tutor,* Disc 2, Chapter 6, Activity 1 to practice describing family members to a partner.

- *Culture* Spanish-speakers often use descriptive **apodos** *(nicknames)* such as **Flaco** *(Skinny)* or **La Rubia** *(The blond one).*

- *Project* Have students draw themselves on poster paper. They write a description of themselves in Spanish with three positive adjectives. For example, **Soy interesante, inteligente y divertido/a.**

Close

- *Game* Divide students into teams. Each team writes five names of well-known people, such as TV or movie stars, on small pieces of paper. A player from Team A picks a piece of paper from Team B and shows it to one other Team A player. The person who chose the paper draws the famous person on a sheet of paper. Once he or she has finished drawing, the teammate who also knows who the celebrity is gives descriptions in Spanish as additional clues, using the vocabulary list. The other members of Team A must guess who it is before the third clue. If Team A guesses correctly, they get another turn. If Team A does not guess correctly, Team B takes a turn. The team with the most correct guesses, wins.

UNIT 8

Activity Master 8.3　　　　　　　　　　　　　　　　　　　　　**Descriptions**

1 Write the name of the person described. Use the blank provided.

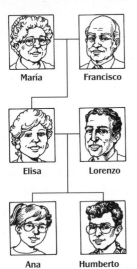

María　　Francisco

Elisa　　Lorenzo

Ana　　Humberto

_____　**1.** Es rubia, inteligente y tiene trece años.

_____　**2.** Es interesante, alto y tiene sesenta y nueve años.

_____　**3.** Es moreno y tiene diecisiete años.

_____　**4.** Es divertido, moreno y tiene cuarenta y dos años.

_____　**5.** Es rubia, simpática y tiene cuarenta años.

_____　**6.** Es inteligente, divertida y tiene sesenta y ocho años.

2 Write a want ad in which you advertise for the ideal friend. Use at least five of the adjectives below to describe the person. Write your ad in the box provided. Use an adjective ending in **-o** for a boy and an adjective ending in **-a** for a girl. When you're finished describing the friend, draw a picture of him or her. Note: **Se busca** means *Looking for.*

bonito/a　　simpático/a　　inteligente　　rubio/a　　moreno/a

divertido/a　　pelirrojo/a　　guapo/a　　interesante

SE BUSCA UN AMIGO/UNA AMIGA

UNIT 8

Unit 8 · Family and Pets   Lesson 4   Pets and Other Animals

¡Ven conmigo! and *Adelante* Resources	Materials you will need
• *Teaching Transparency 6-A*	• Magazine pictures of animals • Index cards with pictures of animals • Blank transparency and transparency marker • Poster paper, scissors, tape or glue

Language and Culture Objectives
Students will

• learn about pets in Latin American countries

• learn vocabulary for pets and other animals

Motivate
• Ask students to discuss whether their pets are considered part of their family. Are some pets more part of the family than others? Do they have nicknames for their pets? How often do they talk with their pets?

Teach
1. *Culture*   Explain that in many Latin American countries pets such as parrots, toucans, monkeys, and iguanas are more common than they are in the United States. These pets are not considered exotic because they are animals native to that area.

2. *Visual Learners*   Display *Teaching Transparency 6-A* to present *cat* and *dog* as you introduce the vocabulary for them in Spanish. Use pictures clipped from magazines to present additional pet and animal vocabulary. Have students repeat the words after you.

3. *Kinesthetic Learners*   Have students work in groups of five. One student draws names of animals from prepared index cards and mime the behavior of the animal. Other students in the group try to guess what animal it is.

4. *Listening*   Have students listen to the Spanish pronunciation of the following animal noises, and write down which animal they think it is. The noises and animals are: **qui-quiri-quí** (chicken); **pío-pío** (bird); **guau guau** (dog); **miau, miau** (cat); **mu** (cow).

5. *Music Link*   Teach students to sing *Mi hermano tiene una finca* to the tune of *Old MacDonald Had a Farm*. Write the words on the board or on a transparency. **"Mi hermano tiene una finca, ¡Ay, el ruido, ay! En su finca hay (una vaca), ¡Ay, el ruido, ay! Con un mu aquí, y un mu allí, por todos lados mu, mu, mu. Mi hermano tiene una finca, ¡Ay, el ruido, ay!"** Continue with the following animals: **un caballo, un gato, un pájaro, un perro, un pato, una gallina.**

6. *Writing*   Have students complete Activity Master 8.4 to practice pet and other animal vocabulary.

Additional Practice
• *Language Learning*   Have students make picture flashcards of vocabulary for pets and other animals.

• *Project*   Have students draw or clip pictures from magazines of pets and barnyard animals. Have them arrange the pictures in a barnyard scene they draw on poster paper. Students label the animals and title the poster **Mi finca** *(My farm)*. Have students draw a picture of a pet or other animal they would like to own if they lived on this farm. Ask students to label the animal and describe some of its characteristics.

Close
• *Game*   Have students work in pairs. First, students write five pet names and the type of animal for each on index cards, without letting their partner see the cards. For example, Spot–dog, Buttercup–cow, Tangerine–fish, and so on. One student says the animal's name; the student guessing may only ask yes-or-no questions to determine what kind of animal it is. For example, —**Tangerine**, —¿**Es un perro?** —No. —¿**Es una vaca?** —No. —**Es un pez?** —**Sí.** If the student is able to guess in fewer than five questions, he or she wins a point.

UNIT 8

Activity Master 8.4   Pets and Other Animals

1 Use the animal vocabulary you've learned to figure out which title goes with which transla-
tion. Write the letter of the English title in the blank provided.

_____ 1. *Un pez, dos peces*   **a.** *The Ugly Duckling*

_____ 2. *La gallinita roja*   **b.** *The Little Red Hen*

_____ 3. *El patito feo*   **c.** *One Fish, Two Fish*

2 Unscramble the following animal names and write the name in the blank. Then match the
animal name with the letter of the correct picture.

MODELO   ___a___ 1. T A O G _____ **gato** _____

_____ 2. Z E P _____

_____ 3. T O P A _____

_____ 4. B A L L A C O _____

_____ 5. L A L A G I N _____

_____ 6. R R O P E _____

_____ 7. J Á R O P A _____

_____ 8. C A V A _____

a

b

c

d

e

f

g

h

Unit 8 · Family and Pets   Vocabulary

LESSON 1 · Family Members

la abuela *grandmother*	el hijo *son*
el abuelo *grandfather*	la madre/mamá *mother/mom*
la familia *family*	el padre/papá *father/dad*
la hermana *sister*	mi *my*
el hermano *brother*	tu *your (familiar)*
la hija *daughter*	

LESSON 2 · Introductions

¿Cómo te llamas? *What's your name?*	Igualmente. *Same here.*
Ésta es... / Éste es... *This is . . .*	Me llamo... *My name is . . .*
Ésta es mi amiga. *This is my friend.*	Mucho gusto. *Nice to meet you.*
(to introduce a female)	
Éste es mi amigo. *This is my friend.*	
(to introduce a male)	

LESSON 3 · Descriptions

¿Cómo es...? *What's . . . like?*	inteligente *intelligent*
alto/a *tall*	interesante *interesting*
antipático/a *disagreeable*	moreno/a *brunette*
bajo/a *short*	pelirrojo/a *redheaded*
divertido/a *fun, amusing*	rubio/a *blond*
Él/Ella es... *He/she is . . .*	simpático/a *nice*
guapo/a *good-looking*	Soy... *I am . . .*

LESSON 4 · Pets and Other Animals

el caballo *horse*	el pato *duck*
la gallina *chicken*	el perro *dog*
el gato *cat*	el pez *fish*
la mascota *pet*	la vaca *cow*
el pájaro *bird*	

UNIT 8

Unit 8 · Family and Pets   Review and Assessment

¡Ven conmigo! and Adelante Resources
- *Teaching Transparency 6-1*
- *Interactive CD-ROM Tutor,* Disc 2

Materials you will need
- Copies of *Teaching Transparency 6-1*
- Project: drawing paper, construction paper, markers, glue or tape, magazines or photos

Language and Culture Objectives
Students will

- show their knowledge of vocabulary for family members, pets, and other animals in Spanish
- show their understanding of families in the Spanish-speaking world
- express their knowledge orally and in the form of an in-class project

Review
1. Have students use a copy of the family tree in *Teaching Transparency 6-1* to review vocabulary for family members. For example, **Éste es el abuelo de Tomás.**
2. Have pairs of students take turns asking and answering **¿Cómo se llama tu hermano/a?**
3. In pairs, have students introduce themselves to each other.
4. Have students take turns describing a friend to a partner.

Assessment Options
Written
- Have students complete **¡Ya lo sé!** for Unit 8. You will find the listening activity script on page 116 of this guide.
- *Project* Have students do a project called **El álbum de mi familia.** First students list their nuclear or extended family using the vocabu-

lary for family members. Allow students to make up an imaginary family for this activity, if they prefer to do so. Then have students draw portraits, use magazine pictures, or bring in photographs of the members of their families for the album. Have students label the pictures or photos and write a brief descriptive sentence in Spanish about each family member, using vocabulary from this unit. For example, **Mi madre es inteligente y simpática.** Students should use at least two adjectives for each descriptive sentence. Have students make a cover for the album and write their name on it as the author.

Oral
1. Ask the student to say the words for three family members in Spanish.
3. Ask the student to respond to an introduction.
4. Ask the student to describe himself or herself in Spanish using two adjectives.
5. Ask the student to name a farm animal in Spanish.
6. Ask the student how many Spanish-speakers affectionately refer to their grandfather or grandmother. (**abuelito, abuelita**)

CD-ROM
- Have students use the *Interactive CD-ROM Tutor,* Disc 2, Chapter 6, Activity 1, to assess students' knowledge of vocabulary for family members.

Unit 8 · Family and Pets   ¡Ya lo sé!   Total Points: 40

A. Family

Listen as Carlos talks about his family. First find
Carlos in the family tree. Write **sí** if his statements
are true and **no** if they are false. (12 points)

1. _____

2. _____

3. _____

4. _____

5. _____

6. _____

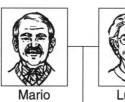

Mario   Luisa

Julio   Rosa

Carlos   Laura   Jaime
(yo)

SCORE _____

B. Introductions

Federico is introducing Teodoro and Luisa to each other. Fill in the blanks in the conversation with words from the word box. (12 points)

Mucho gusto	Ésta es	Me llamo	Cómo te llamas

FEDERICO   Hola, Teodoro, ¿cómo estás?

TEODORO   Regular, ¿y tú?

FEDERICO   Muy bien. **1.** _____ mi amiga Luisa.

TEODORO   Mucho gusto, Luisa.

LUISA   **2.** ¿_____?

TEODORO   **3.** _____ Teodoro.

LUISA   **4.** _____, Teodoro.

TEODORO   Hasta luego, Luisa y Federico.

FEDERICO   Adiós.

SCORE _____

Unit 8 · Family and Pets   ¡Ya lo sé!   *Continued*

C. Descriptions

Match the sentences with the pictures they describe. Write the letter of the picture in the space provided. (10 points)

_____ 1. Mi mascota es muy divertida.

_____ 2. Rubén es alto y rubio y Dinora es baja y morena.

_____ 3. El hermano de Santiago es moreno y tiene doce años.

_____ 4. La abuela de mi amigo Juan es muy simpática.

_____ 5. Mi hermana es inteligente y rubia.

a

b

c

d

e

SCORE _____

D. Saludos *(Greetings)*

Match the following pictures with the sentences that describe them. (6 points)

a

b

c

_____ 1. My brother's friend

_____ 2. My father's friend

_____ 3. My close friend

SCORE _____

TOTAL SCORE _____ /40

Unit 9 · Clothes and the Body　　　Lesson 1　　　Clothing

¡Ven conmigo! and Adelante/En camino Resources

- *Teaching Transparencies 9-C* and *9-D*
- *Interactive CD-ROM Tutor,* Disc 3

Materials you will need

- Clothing items from vocabulary list
- Paper, scissors
- Colored pens or paints
- Clothing catalogs, magazines, newspaper

Language and Culture Objectives

Students will

- learn cultural information about uniforms
- learn phrases to talk about clothing

Motivate

- Discuss school uniforms with students. What do students think about the idea of wearing uniforms to school? Do they or any of their friends wear uniforms? What are the advantages and the disadvantages? Tell students that schools in Spanish-speaking countries commonly require students to wear uniforms.

Teach

1. *Culture* Different cultures have different norms about how to dress. In many Spanish-speaking countries it is not considered appropriate to wear shorts or sport clothes except in places where people exercise. In the United States, on the other hand, people frequently jog downtown, wearing running shorts and T-shirts. Also, many people in the U.S. wear sport clothes even if they are not exercising. As a rule, people in Spanish-speaking countries dress more formally and take great pride in their personal appearance. Some even iron jeans and T-shirts!

2. *Visual Learners* Display *Teaching Transparencies 9-C* and *9-D* to present clothing vocabulary to students. Have students draw, paint, or clip pictures from clothing magazines to make their ideal school uniform. This can be done as a game, with an award going to the silliest uniform, or as a regular learning activity.

3. *Listening* Have students stand. Call out clothing vocabulary. Each student who is wearing the article of clothing points to it.

For example, say **los calcetines** and have students wearing socks point to them.

4. *Kinesthetic Learners* Bring clothes from the vocabulary list to school. Divide the class in half. Have students from different teams face off, game-show style, one-on-one. Hold up the article of clothing, and whichever team is first to name it correctly "wins" that item. At the end, the team with the most items wins.

5. *Writing* Have students complete Activity Master 9.1 to practice vocabulary for clothing.

Additional Practice

- *Visual Learners* Have students use the *Interactive CD-ROM Tutor,* Disc 3, Chapter 9, Activity 4 to practice clothing vocabulary.

- *Project* Divide the class into pairs. Assign each pair two vocabulary words at random. Students pretend they work for an advertising agency, and their job is to create a newspaper ad for the two types of clothing. They may draw the ad, or cut and paste from newspapers and magazines.

Close

- *Game* Have students wrap clothing items in newspaper. Collect the packages. Have students put their hands behind their backs. Put one package on each desk. Anyone who touches a package is out of the game. One at a time students guess what is inside their package. Each student can make three guesses before opening the package. The student who guesses incorrectly loses the package, rewraps it and puts it on a table in the front of the room. The next student who guesses correctly "wins" all the extra packages on the table. Students continue guessing, and the one with the most packages at the end wins.

Activity Master 9.1   Clothing

1 Match the Spanish word with the correct picture.

_____ **1.** las sandalias

_____ **2.** la camisa

_____ **3.** la chaqueta

_____ **4.** el traje de baño

_____ **5.** los pantalones

_____ **6.** la falda

_____ **7.** la camiseta

_____ **8.** el vestido

ⓐ   **ⓑ**   **ⓒ**   **ⓓ**

ⓔ   **ⓕ**   **ⓖ**   **ⓗ**

2 In the space provided write the Spanish word that answers the question.

> **unas botas**   **un suéter**   **unos calcetines**   **una chaqueta**   **un vestido**
> **un traje de baño**   **una camisa**   **un cinturón**   **unas sandalias**   **una camiseta**

1. What do you wear to keep your pants up? _____

2. What kind of shoes do cowboys wear? _____

3. What do you wear to go swimming? _____

4. What kind of shirt do you wear to a wedding? _____

5. What kind of shirt do you wear to play basketball? _____

6. What kind of shoes are only for summer? _____

7. What do girls wear to their high school prom? _____

8. What hand-knit item is for chilly weather? _____

9. What do you put on to go outside when it's cold? _____

10. If you wore one red one, and one blue one people might laugh. What are they?

_____

UNIT 9

Unit 9 · Clothes and the Body   Lesson 2   Shopping

¡Ven conmigo! and *Adelante/En camino* Resources
- *Teaching Transparency 9-3*
- *Video Program* and *Video Guide,* Chapter 9

Materials you will need
- Index cards
- Clothing items from the vocabulary list

Language and Culture Objectives
Students will
- learn about shopping in outdoor markets
- learn phrases to use when shopping for clothing

Motivate
- Discuss what kinds of clothes you might find in Mexico, Puerto Rico, or Ecuador, and how they might vary due to climate and culture. Ask students what they think sixth graders wear in those countries. Write students' descriptions on the board and compare.

Teach
1. *Culture*   Sometimes Americans make the mistake of trying to bargain at the wrong places when visiting other countries. Generally, vendors expect people to bargain with them in outdoor markets. Bargaining is an art form in these markets; a successful shopper may bring the price down to half of the original offer. However, bargaining is not appropriate when shopping in indoor shops, such as department stores.

2. *Visual Learners*   Display *Teaching Transparency 9-3* of people trying on clothes in a store. Give students examples of prices and expressions to describe them. For example, if it's a bargain people say **¡Es una ganga!** Have students repeat the phrases after you.

3. *Language Learning*   Have students make and use flashcards to practice clothing and shopping-related expressions.

4. *Listening*   Hold up a clothing item and name a price in Spanish. Students hold up their **¡Qué caro!** flashcards if the price is high, **¡Qué barato!** if it's low. After a few examples, they switch to their **¡Es un robo!** and **¡Es una ganga!** flashcards. Then name prices and have students respond aloud.

5. *Speaking*   Display *Teaching Transparency 9-3.* Have students pretend they are shopping and discuss in Spanish whether the prices in the store are a good deal. For example, one partner says **Una falda cuesta diez dólares** and the other says **¡Es una ganga!**

6. *Writing*   Have students complete Activity Master 9.2 to practice vocabulary used while shopping.

Additional Practice
- *Visual Learners*   Play the **De antemano** video for Chapter 9 without sound. Pause on the clothes shopping scene and have students guess from the facial gestures whether the clothes are **una ganga** or **un robo.**

- *Project*   Divide students into teams of four. Pass several articles of clothing to each team. Each team prepares a skit in which two are salespeople and the other two are shoppers. The shoppers ask **¿Cuánto cuesta?** and the salespeople answer **Cuesta...** The shoppers respond with **¡Qué barato!** or **¡Qué caro!** Give students time to prepare and practice, and then ask them to perform their skits.

Close
- *Game*   Divide the class into six groups and assign each a phrase from this lesson's vocabulary. For example, **¿Cuánto cuesta?** for Group 1, **¡Es un robo!** for Group 2, **¡Es una ganga!** for Group 3, **¡Qué barato!** for Group 4, and **¡Qué caro!** for Group 5. Hold up an item of clothing. Group 1 stands, says **¿Cuánto cuesta?,** and sits down. Pretend to model the clothing. Group 6 stands and says **Te queda muy bien,** and sits down. Name a price in dollars. Then students from Groups 2 to 5 stand and say their phrase if they think it applies. If two groups with the opposite phrases stand, then students discuss why the price is **una ganga** or **un robo.**

UNIT 9

Activity Master 9.2   **Shopping**

1 Write the prices of the clothes pictured below in numerals in the space provided.

1. la camiseta _____   5. el suéter _____

2. el vestido _____   6. la camisa _____

3. la chaqueta _____   7. el cinturón _____

4. las sandalias _____

2 **¿Es una ganga o un robo?** Check **¡Es una ganga!** if the price is *a bargain* and **¡Es un robo!** if the price is too much.

	¡Es una ganga!	¡Es un robo!
1. un cinturón por $60		
2. unas botas por $10		
3. un vestido por $3		
4. unas sandalias por $2		
5. una falda por $120		
6. un suéter por $2		
7. unos pantalones cortos por $74		
8. unos pantalones por $4		

UNIT 9

Unit 9 · Clothes and the Body   Lesson 3   The Body

¡Ven conmigo! and Adelante/En camino Resources

- *Teaching Transparency 11-C*
- *Interactive CD-ROM Tutor,* Disc 3

Materials you will need

- Paper, markers or colored pencils
- Magazines, scissors, tape or glue

Language and Culture Objectives

Students will

- learn cultural information about the words for fingers, toes, and feet
- learn vocabulary for parts of the body

Motivate

- Discuss physical fitness. What do students do for exercise? Do they play sports? What do they like to do outdoors?

Teach

1. *Culture*   In Spanish, the word **dedos** means both *fingers* and *toes.* Normally the context will clarify which meaning is intended. If not, people may say **dedo del pie** to clarify they mean *toe.* Like English, Spanish has certain words for human parts of the body, and other terms for animal parts of the body. The word for a human foot is **pie**, and the word for an animal foot is **pata**.

2. *Visual and Kinesthetic Learners*   Show students *Teaching Transparency 11-C* of two gymnasts with the parts of the body labeled in Spanish. Have students stand and point to their head, eyes, mouth, nose, and so on, and say the word for it in Spanish as you present the vocabulary. Then teach students a song to the tune of *Twinkle, Twinkle Little Star.* Have students touch the respective body parts and sing the lyrics, **Cabeza, brazos, piernas, pies. Cabeza, brazos, piernas, pies. Ojos, oídos, boca, nariz. Ojos, oídos, boca, nariz. Cabeza, brazos, piernas, pies. Cabeza, brazos, piernas, pies.**

3. *Listening*   Have students work in groups of eleven. As you call out words for parts of the body, students draw them. Begin with **la cabeza.** Each student in the group draws a circle or an oval for a head at the top of the paper and passes it to the person on the left. Students pass the drawing on and in succession draw a nose, eyes, a mouth, ears, a neck, the body, the arms, the hands, the legs, and the feet.

4. *Kinesthetic Learners*   Play **Simón dice** *(Simon Says)* to reinforce vocabulary for parts of the body. Remind students that they only follow the instructions when you say **Simón dice.** Have students stand. Give directions, for example, **Simón dice: Toquen la boca.** However, when you say **Toquen la cabeza,** students who touch their head must sit down. The last student standing is the winner.

5. *Writing*   Have students complete Activity Master 9.3 to practice words in Spanish for parts of the body.

Additional Practice

- *Visual Learners*   Have students use the *Interactive CD-ROM Tutor,* Disc 3, Chapter 11, Activity 4, to practice recognizing vocabulary for parts of the body. Tell students that **el pelo** is *hair* and **las orejas** are *ears.*

- *Project*   Have students cut out a full-length picture of a person from a magazine and paste it onto paper. Next, students use a ruler to draw lines and label all the parts of the body on the vocabulary list. Give students extra points for identifying: **el codo** *(elbow),* **la rodilla** *(knee),* **los hombros** *(shoulders),* **el tobillo** *(ankle),* and **el ombligo** *(belly button).*

Close

- *Game*   Divide the class in half to play a word guessing game. Draw blanks for the number of letters. For example: _ _ _ _ _ _ **(la boca).** A student from Team 1 calls out a letter in Spanish. If the team guesses correctly, the teacher draws a stick-figure head and another student from their team guesses a letter. If the student guesses incorrectly, Team 2 gets a turn. The first team to get a complete stick figure drawn wins.

UNIT 9

Activity Master 9.3   The Body

1 First unscramble the words below. Then match each part of the body in the diagram with the correct Spanish word. One label will be used twice.

MODELO ___l___ 1. earinp _____**pierna**_____

_____ 2. coba _____

_____ 3. namo _____

_____ 4. razin _____

_____ 5. sdode _____

_____ 6. sooj _____

_____ 7. magóesto _____

_____ 8. zabeca _____

_____ 9. ipe _____

_____ 10. plasdea _____

_____ 11. dosoí _____

_____ 12. zobra _____

_____ 13. louelc _____

_____ 14. narpie _____

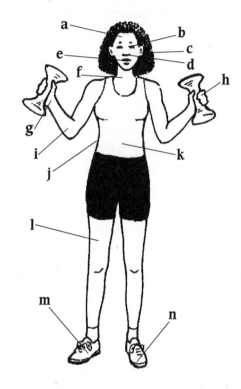

2 What parts of the body do you use in these activities? Name one or two of them in Spanish for each item.

1. skating _____

2. cooking dinner _____

3. dancing _____

4. drawing _____

5. talking on the phone _____

6. swimming _____

7. singing _____

8. skiing _____

9. listening to music _____

10. reading _____

Unit 9 · Clothes and the Body   Lesson 4   Health

¡Ven conmigo! and Adelante/En camino Resources

- *Teaching Transparency 11-B*
- *Interactive CD-ROM Tutor, Disc 3*

Materials you will need

- Index cards, magazines, scissors
- Thermometer, facial tissue, cough syrup, can of chicken soup
- Poster board, tape or glue

Language and Culture Objectives

Students will

- learn cultural information about health traditions
- learn phrases to discuss their health

Motivate

- Ask students what they do to keep from getting sick. For example, do they wear hats in the winter? Ask students what they do when they feel sick.

Teach

1. ***Culture*** Many Latin Americans don't drink very cold drinks and tend not to put ice in lemonade, water, and soft drinks because they consider cold drinks harmful to the body. In very warm weather, many people drink fluids that are room temperature to maintain a constant body temperature. Traditional wisdom holds that cold drinks cool the body momentarily, but soon make the person feel even warmer.

2. ***Visual Learners*** Display *Teaching Transparency 11-B* to present vocabulary to talk about feelings and health. Have students repeat the words after you. Have them make vocabulary flashcards with drawings or pictures clipped from magazines of people who represent the vocabulary.

3. ***Kinesthetic Learning*** Bring in a thermometer (to model having a fever), facial tissue (to model having a cold), cough syrup (to model having a cough), a can of chicken soup (to model having the flu), and various other items (magazine, telephone, book, etc.). Pass out items to students. Say the vocabulary about health, such as **Tengo fiebre,** and have the student with the thermometer raise his or her hand.

4. ***Speaking*** Have students work with partners. They imagine one partner is having a very bad day and the other is having a great day. The partner who is having a good day asks the other how he or she is doing: **¿Cómo estás?** The partner gives three or four reasons why the day is not going well, for example, **Estoy mal. Tengo fiebre y estoy resfriado. Tengo gripe.** Then partners switch roles.

5. ***Writing*** Have students complete Activity Master 9.4 to practice vocabulary related to feelings and health.

Additional Practice

- ***Culture*** When someone sneezes in a Spanish-speaking country, people wish them good health by responding, **¡Salud!** Some Spanish-speakers have a series of sayings they use when a person sneezes several times. The first time someone sneezes they say **¡Salud!** *(Health!)*. The second time they say **¡Amor!** *(Love!)* and for the third they say **¡Dinero!** *(Wealth! or Money!)*. If someone sneezes a fourth time, they say **¡Y tiempo para gozarlos!** *(And time to enjoy them!)*. Ask students what they say when someone sneezes.

- ***Visual*** Have students use the *Interactive CD-ROM Tutor,* Disc 3, Chapter 11, Activity 3 to practice recognizing health vocabulary.

- ***Project*** Have students make a poster of four health vocabulary words. Have them draw or clip pictures from magazines that represent things they associate with being sick, having a fever, having a cold, and so on.

Close

- ***Game*** Have students play charades to practice vocabulary for health and feelings.

UNIT 9

Activity Master 9.4   **Health**

1 What would you say in Spanish if the following happened? Match the correct Spanish phrase with the English description. One phrase will be used twice.

_____ **1.** If you can't breathe through your nose . . .   **a.** Estoy triste.

_____ **2.** If you have a fever . . .   **b.** Tengo gripe.

_____ **3.** If you're feeling sad . . .   **c.** Tengo tos.

_____ **4.** If you have a cough . . .   **d.** Tengo fiebre.

_____ **5.** If you have the flu . . .   **e.** Estoy resfriado./Estoy resfriada.

_____ **6.** If your best friend just moved away . . .

2 Complete the crossword puzzle. Use the pictures as the crossword clues for what the people pictured would say about their health or feelings.

Unit 9 · Clothes and the Body   Vocabulary

LESSON 1 · Clothing

los bluejeans *blue jeans*
las botas *boots*
los calcetines *socks*
la camisa *shirt*
la camiseta *T-shirt*
la chaqueta *jacket*
el cinturón *belt*

la falda *skirt*
los pantalones *pants*
los pantalones cortos *shorts*
las sandalias *sandals*
el suéter *sweater*
el traje de baño *bathing suit*
el vestido *dress*

LESSON 2 · Shopping

¿Cuánto cuesta...? *How much does . . .
cost?*
¡Es un robo! *It's a rip-off!*
¡Es una ganga! *It's a bargain!*

¡Qué barato! *How cheap!*
¡Qué caro! *How expensive!*
Te queda muy bien. *It looks good on you.*

LESSON 3 · The Body

la boca *mouth*
el brazo *arm*
la cabeza *head*
el cuello *neck*
el cuerpo *body*
el dedo *finger, toe*
la espalda *back*

el estómago *stomach*
la mano *hand*
la nariz *nose*
el oído *ear*
el ojo *eye*
el pie *foot*
la pierna *leg*

LESSON 4 · Health

¿Cómo estás? *How are you?*
Estoy mal. *I feel bad.*
Estoy triste. *I'm sad.*
Estoy resfriado/a. *I have a cold.*

Tengo fiebre. *I have a fever.*
Tengo gripe. *I have the flu.*
Tengo tos. *I have a cough.*

UNIT 9

Unit 9 · Clothes and the Body   **Review and Assessment**

¡Ven conmigo! and *Adelante/En camino* **Resources**

- *Interactive CD-ROM Tutor,* Disc 3

Materials you will need

- Vocabulary flashcards
- Drawing paper, pencils or pens

Language and Culture Assessment Objectives

Students will

- show their knowledge of vocabulary for clothes, body, and health in Spanish
- show their knowledge of culture in the Spanish-speaking world
- express their knowledge orally and in the form of an in-class project

Review

1. Call out clothing items and have students hold up the correct flashcard.

2. Have students sing *Cabeza, brazos, piernas, pies* from Lesson 3, page 101.

3. Have students review the names of parts of the body with a partner. For example, one partner says **el brazo,** and the other student points to his or her arm.

4. Have one partner say a price and the other respond in Spanish. For example, one says **La chaqueta cuesta cinco dólares.** The other student responds **¡Qué barato!**

5. Have students ask each other **¿Cómo estás?** in pairs and respond by miming an illness and making an appropriate statement.

Assessment Options

Written

- Have students complete **¡Ya lo sé!,** Unit 9. You will find the script for the listening activity on page 116 of this guide.

- *Project* Have pairs of students trace each other's outlines on a large sheets of paper. Students draw clothes and label the clothes and the parts of the body in Spanish.

Oral

1. Ask the student **¿Cómo estás?** and have the student answer, pretending he or she is ill.

2. Place five pictures of clothing on the desk for the student to identify.

3. Ask the student to point to the article of clothing you mention, for example, **las sandalias** or **los calcetines.**

4. Say an exaggerated price for an article of clothing and have the student respond with an exclamation in Spanish. For example, **La camisa cuesta tres dólares. ¡Es una ganga!**

5. Ask the student what type of clothing Spanish-speaking students often wear to school (a uniform) or if they should offer an ice-cold drink to someone from Latin America. (Many Latin Americans don't think iced drinks are healthy.)

CD-ROM

- Have students use the *Interactive CD-ROM Tutor,* Disc 3, Chapter 9, Activity 4 to review clothing vocabulary and Chapter 11, Activity 4 to review vocabulary for parts of the body.

Nombre _____ Clase _____ Fecha _____

Unit 9 · Clothes and the Body   ¡Ya lo sé!   Total Points: 40

A. The Body
Match the parts of the body you hear with the letters on the drawing. (16 points)

1. _____

2. _____

3. _____

4. _____

5. _____

6. _____

7. _____

8. _____

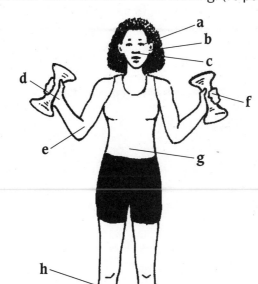

B. Clothing
Match the name of the clothing in Spanish with the picture of the person wearing it. (12 points)

  a   **b**   **c**   **d**

_____ 1. una falda

_____ 2. unos pantalones cortos

_____ 3. unas sandalias

_____ 4. un traje de baño

_____ 5. unos pantalones

_____ 6. una camisa

SCORE

UNIT 9

Unit 9 · Clothes and the Body ¡Ya lo sé! *continued*

C. Shopping

What are two expressions that would fit each of the following situations? Match each
expression with the price it describes. (8 points)

_____ , _____ 1. —¿Cuánto cuesta el cinturón?

—Cuesta $75.00.

_____ , _____ 2. —¿Cuánto cuesta la camiseta?

—Cuesta $2.00.

a. ¡Es un robo!   b. ¡Qué barato!   c. ¡Qué caro!   d. ¡Es una ganga!

SCORE [   ]

D. La cultura

Write **cierto** if a statement is *true* and **falso** if it is *false.* (4 points)

_____ 1.   _____ 2.

People don't bargain in open-air markets
in Latin America.

Students in Spanish-speaking countries
usually wear uniforms.

SCORE [   ]

TOTAL SCORE [/40]

UNIT 1

Activity Master 1.1, p. 2

1 Central America (North to South):
7. Guatemala; 4. El Salvador;
2. Honduras; 6. Nicaragua;
8. Costa Rica; 9. Panamá

Caribbean Islands (West to East):
5. Cuba; 1. República Dominicana;
3. Puerto Rico

2

G	U	I	N	E	A	E	C	U	A	T	O	R	I	A	L	B	
																O	
		C	H	I	L	E										L	
						E	C	U	A	D	O	R	I			I	
				P	U	E	R	T	O	R	I	C	O			V	
U	V								L							I	P
R	E	P	Ú	B	L	I	C	A	D	O	M	I	N	I	C	A	N	A
U	N	E							M							A	R
G	E	R							B				M			A	A
U	Z	Ú							I				É			G	
A	U								A				X			U	
Y	E			E	S	P	A	Ñ	A	R	G	E	N	T	I	N	A
	L												C			A	Y
	A												O				

Activity Master 1.2, p. 4

1 1. Texas; 2. Cuba; 3. Perú; 4. Miami;
5. España

2 1. helicóptero; 2. león; 3. rosa; 4. trompeta; 5. serpiente; 6. arte; 7. cebra

3 *Answers will vary.*

Activity Master 1.3, p. 6

1 México

2 1; 6; 20; 15; 9; 17

3
1. dos	5. trece	8. doce
2. tres	6. ocho	9. diez
3. cuatro	7. siete	10. cero
4. cinco		

4
1. seis	5. nueve	8. uno
2. quince	6. dieciséis	9. catorce
3. veinte	7. tres	10. once
4. dieciocho		

Activity Master 1.4, p. 8

1 3 red and 2 white stripes, blue triangle, and white star

2 1. amarillo; 2. azul; 3. *Answers will vary. Possible answers:* rojo, anaranjado, amarillo, marrón, verde; 4. verde; 5. morado;
6. rojo *or* anaranjado; 7. blanco; 8. negro

3 Mosaic colors beginning at the twelve o'clock position and going clockwise: blue, red, gray, purple, white, black, yellow, green.

UNIT 2

Activity Master 2.1, p. 14

1 1. c   2. a   3. b
2 1. a   2. b   3. a   4. c   5. a
3 1. a   2. b   3. a   4. a   5. b

Activity Master 2.2, p. 16

1 Question: ¿Cuántos años tienes?;
1. d   2. c   3. a   4. b

2 1. Cuatro más quince son diecinueve.
2. Doce más catorce son veintiséis.
3. Once más trece son veinticuatro.
4. Treinta y seis más veinticuatro son sesenta.
5. Cuarenta y cinco más siete son cincuenta y dos.

3 *Answers will vary. Possible answers:*
1. Tiene cinco años.
2. Tiene dieciocho años.
3. Tiene once años.
4. Tiene trece años.

Activity Master 2.3, p. 18

1 *Answers will vary. Possible answers:*
Las clases
1. Me gusta la clase de español.
2. No me gusta la tarea.
Los deportes
3. Me gusta el voleibol.
4. No me gusta el baloncesto.

2
1. SAMUEL   ¿**Te** gusta el tenis?
    FRANCISCO   A mí no **me gusta** el tenis.
2. SAMUEL   ¿**Te** gusta la natación?
    FRANCISCO   A mí **me gusta** mucho la natación.
3. FRANCISCO   A mí **me gusta** el béisbol.
    SAMUEL   Pues a mí no me gusta **el béisbol**.
4. SAMUEL   ¿**Te gusta** el baloncesto?
    FRANCISCO   ¡Sí, me gusta muchísimo!

Activity Master 2.4, p. 20

1 pizza; fruta; años; música; béisbol; ensalada; voleibol; **Solución:** español

2
1. el chocolate	4. la tarea
2. la natación	5. el español
3. la comida italiana	

3 *Answers will vary. Possible answers:*
1. No me gusta el fútbol norteamericano.
2. Me gusta la música jazz.

UNIT 3
Activity Master 3.1, p. 26

1 1. Eduardo   3. Rafael   5. Rosita
2. Lola   4. Miguel

2 1. el cuaderno   6. el diccionario
2. la regla   7. la mochila
3. la carpeta   8. el papel
4. la goma de borrar   9. la librería
5. el marcador   10. el libro

Activity Master 3.2, p. 28

1 1. c   2. d   3. b   4. a
2 4:00; 1:00; 3:15; 10:00
3 1. Son las doce y cuarto.
2. Son las seis.
3. Son las siete y media.

Activity Master 3.3, p. 30

1 a. lunes   c. jueves   e. sábado
b. miércoles   d. viernes   f. domingo
Monday, **lunes,** begins the week in
Spanish-speaking countries.

2 a. sábado (#6)   d. martes (#2)
b. jueves (#4)   e. domingo (#7)
c. miércoles (#3)   f. viernes (#5)

Activity Master 3.4, p. 32

1 1. geografía
2. educación física
3. computación
4. matemáticas
5. arte
6. francés; Ángela's favorite class is **ciencias.**

2 1. e   2. f   3. d   4. a   5. b   6. c

UNIT 4
Activity Master 4.1, p. 38

1 1. c   2. a   3. b
2 *Answers will vary. Possible answers:*
1. Me gusta jugar al voleibol.
2. No me gusta jugar al tenis.
3. Me gusta jugar al fútbol.

Activity Master 4.2, p. 40

1 1. c   2. a   3. d   4. b
2 1. e   2. c   3. a   4. b   5. d
Sí and No: *Answers will vary.*

Activity Master 4.3, p. 42

1 1. b   2. c   3. a
2 *Answers will vary. Possible answers:*
1. Me gusta dibujar.
2. Me gusta cantar.
3. Me gusta hablar por teléfono.
4. Me gusta pasar el rato con amigos.

3 *Answers will vary. Possible answers:*
1. Sí, me gustaría escuchar música un poco.
2. No, no me gustaría para nada.
3. Sí, me gustaría mucho.

Activity Master 4.4, p. 44

1 *Answers will vary. Possible answers:*
1. No me gusta nadar porque es difícil.
2. Me gusta esquiar porque es interesante.
3. Me gusta patinar en línea porque es divertido.

2 1. b   2. b   3. b

UNIT 5
Activity Master 5.1, p. 50

1 1. Hace viento.   5. Hace frío.
2. Está nevando.   6. Está lloviendo.
3. Hace fresco.   7. Está nublado.
4. Hace mucho calor.   8. Hace sol.

2 1. En Phoenix hace sol.
2. En San Francisco está lloviendo.
3. En Minneapolis está nevando.

Activity Master 5.2, p. 52

1 a. junio, 6   g. julio, 7
b. febrero, 2   h. noviembre, 11
c. agosto, 8   i. marzo, 3
d. septiembre, 9   j. mayo, 5
e. octubre, 10   k. diciembre, 12
f. enero, 1   l. abril, 4

2 1. f   2. d   3. b   4. a   5. c   6. e
3 1. 26/7   3. 8/4   5. 12/11
2. 27/2   4. 14/9   6. 19/6

Activity Master 5.3, p. 54

1 *Answers will vary. Possible answers:*
1. es el otoño. Hace fresco.; 2. es el verano.
Hace sol.; 3. es la primavera. Está
lloviendo.; 4. es el invierno. Está
nevando.; 5. es la primavera. Hace viento.;
6. es el verano. Hace mucho calor.

2 1. d   2. a   3. c   4. b

Activity Master 5.4, p. 56

1 1. cuatro de julio; 2. ... de noviembre;
3. catorce de febrero; 4. primero de enero;
5. *Answers will vary.*

2 *Answers will vary. Possible answers:*
1. Para el Día de los Enamorados me gusta
bailar.; 2. Para el Día de Acción de Gracias
me gusta comer.; 3. Para la Nochevieja me
gusta mirar la televisión.; 4. Para mi
cumpleaños me gusta cantar.

3 1. el Día de los Enamorados; 2. el Día de
las Madres; 3. el Día de la Independencia;
4. el Día de Acción de Gracias

Answers to Activity Masters, Units 6 and 7

UNIT 6

Activity Master 6.1, p. 62

1 1. e 2. c 3. b 4. f 5. d 6. a

2
```
L B A P U E S E A C A C E R F I N
U I N A A E C U A M O R Á L U C L
G A C N Í H J S E E I T Ú C L O T
I N U G L A T E T U A P A N Ñ S O
J U C S D E N A R A N J A L O E C
V C E O A C I Ñ L O S A N L N R I
N E I T H U E V O S P D O X A E N
E R D H S E U H O F D U U Y A A O
Z E A J F R U T A P E L T J L T
U A R O P L Á T A N O R C A Í R U
L L R U G U X A N P Y O E I Q G Y
```

3 *Answers will vary.*

Activity Master 6.2, p. 64

1 **Sandwiches:** sándwich de atún, sándwich de crema de maní
Fruit: plátano, manzana
Soups: sopa de pollo
Drinks: leche, refresco, té frío

2 1. Lupe 2. Sebastián 3. Victoria

Activity Master 6.3, p. 66

1 1. Sofía 2. Marimar 3. Manuel

2 *Answers will vary. Possible answers:*
Meat: bistec, pollo
Vegetable: ensalada, papas fritas, zanahorias
Beverage: leche, té frío
Dessert: pastel, fruta

Activity Master 6.4, p. 68

1 1. C 4. S 7. C
2. C 5. C 8. C
3. S 6. S

2
CAMARERO	¿**Qué** quiere usted, señora?
SEÑORA VILLANUEVA	**Quisiera** el pollo, las zanahorias, y el arroz.
CAMARERO	¿Y para **beber**, señora?
SEÑORA VILLANUEVA	**Quisiera** el té frío.
CAMARERO	¿Qué **quiere** usted, señor?
SEÑOR VILLANUEVA	Quisiera el bistec, las papas fritas y un refresco. Y, ¿**me puede** traer una servilleta?

UNIT 7

Activity Master 7.1, p. 74

1 1. Voy a la biblioteca.
2. Voy a la piscina.
3. Voy a la tienda./Voy al supermercado.
4. Voy al correo.
5. Voy al cine.

2
```
                    7.
                    E
            1. E L A P I S C I N A
                    G
         2. L A B I B L I O T E C A
                    M
     5.             N                    9.      10.
  3. E L R E S T A U R A N T E    E       L
     C              S                    L       A
     A              I         8.         C       T
     S              O         E          O       I
     A  6.          E L       L          R       E
     A  4. E L C I N E L S U P E R M E R C A D O
         C                    P          O       D
         I                    A                  A
         N                    R
         E                    Q
                              U
                              E
```

Activity Master 7.2, p. 76

1 1. d 2. a 3. b 4. c

2 1. Parque Pista/Parque Valdivia/Gran Plaza
2. Museo de arte
3. Correo
4. Restaurante Nueva York

Activity Master 7.3, p. 78

1 1. c 2. a 3. b 4. e

2 The tapestry has a green snake pattern.

Activity Master 7.4, p. 80

1 1. cocodrillo 6. tigre
2. mono 7. cebra
3. tortuga 8. león
4. loro 9. elefante
5. serpiente 10. oso

2 1. *Answers will vary according to year.* Subtract 100 from the current year.
2. They eat grass, leaves, and cactus.
3. *Answers will vary. Possible answers:* Three of the following: rats, cats, pigs, humans, donkeys, goats, and cattle.

Answers to Activity Masters, Units 8 and 9

UNIT 8

Activity Master 8.1, p. 86

1
1. la hija   4. la madre
2. el padre   5. el abuelo
3. la hermana

2 **Male:** abuelo, padre, hijo, hermano;
Female: abuela, madre, hija, hermana

Activity Master 8.2, p. 88

1
1. SAMUEL   Hola, me llamo Samuel.
2. RIGOBERTA   Hola, Samuel.
3. SAMUEL   ¿Cómo **te llamas**?
4. RIGOBERTA   **Me llamo** Rigoberta.
5. SAMUEL   **Mucho gusto,** Rigoberta.
6. RIGOBERTA   **Igualmente.** Hasta mañana.
7. SAMUEL   Adiós.

2 1. b   2. a   3. c   4. b
3 1. c   2. d   3. b   4. a

Activity Master 8.3, p. 90

1
1. Ana   4. Lorenzo
2. Francisco   5. Elisa
3. Humberto   6. María

2 *Answers will vary.*

Activity Master 8.4, p. 92

1 1. c   2. b   3. a

2
1. gato, a   4. caballo, e   7. pájaro, f
2. pez, c   5. gallina, g   8. vaca, h
3. pato, d   6. perro, b

UNIT 9

Activity Master 9.1, p. 98

1
1. b   4. a   7. e
2. d   5. g   8. c
3. f   6. h

2
1. un cinturón   6. unas sandalias
2. unas botas   7. un vestido
3. un traje de baño   8. un suéter
4. una camisa   9. una chaqueta
5. una camiseta   10. unos calcetines

Activity Master 9.2, p. 100

1
1. $9   4. $30   6. $30
2. $99   5. $27   7. $22
3. $248

2 ¡Es una ganga!: 2, 3, 4, 6, 8
¡Es un robo!: 1, 5, 7

Activity Master 9.3, p. 102

1
1. pierna, l   8. cabeza, a
2. boca, e   9. pie, m
3. mano, g   10. espalda, j
4. nariz, d   11. oídos, c
5. dedos, h, n   12. brazo, i
6. ojos, b   13. cuello, f
7. estómago, k   14. pierna, l

2
1. las piernas, los pies
2. las manos, los dedos
3. las piernas, los pies, los brazos
4. las manos, los dedos de la mano
5. la boca
6. las piernas, los pies, los brazos, las manos
7. la boca, los oídos
8. las piernas, los pies, los brazos, las manos
9. los oídos
10. los ojos

Activity Master 9.4, p. 104

1 1. e   2. d   3. a   4. c   5. b   6. a

2

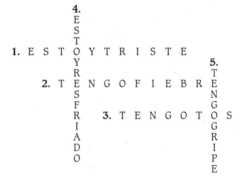

Scripts and Answers for ¡Ya lo sé!, Units 1–3

UNIT 1 ¡Ya lo sé!

Script

A. The Alphabet
1. a-u-ese-te-ere-a-ele-i-a (Australia)
2. u-ere-u-ge-u-a-i griega (Uruguay)
3. ce-hache-i-ene-a (China)
4. pe-e-ere-u (Perú)
5. hache-o-ene-de-u-ere-a-ese (Honduras)

Answers (40 points total)

A. The Alphabet (10 points: 2 points per item)
1. Australia   4. Perú
2. Uruguay   5. Honduras
3. China

B. Colors (10 points: 2 points per item)
1. negro, blanco
2. amarillo
3. anaranjado
4. rojo
5. verde

C. Numbers (16 points: 2 points per item)
1. 10   5. dieciocho
2. 7   6. catorce
3. 13   7. dos
4. 6   8. nueve

D. El español (4 points: 1 point per item)
See map on *¡Ven conmigo!*, page T30 or *Adelante*, page T28. Four of the following countries: Ecuador, Chile, Paraguay, Uruguay, Argentina, Bolivia, Colombia, Perú, Venezuela.

Unit 2 ¡Ya lo sé!

Script

A. Likes and Dislikes
1. A mí me gusta el fútbol.
2. No me gusta el tenis, me gusta el baloncesto.
3. Me gusta la natación.
4. Me gusta la clase de español.
5. ¿Te gusta la comida china?

Answers (40 points total)

A. Likes and Dislikes (10 points: 2 per item)
1. sí   3. no   5. no
2. no   4. sí

B. La quinceañera (4 points: 2 per item)
1. 15   2. b

C. How old are you? (16 points: 4 points for the first question, then 3 points each)
Question: ¿Cuántos años tienes?
1. d   3. a
2. b   4. c

D. How are you? (10 points: 2 per item)
1. a   4. c
2. c   5. a
3. b

Unit 3 ¡Ya lo sé!

Script

A. School Supplies

CLARA   No tengo bolígrafo y no tengo libro. Pero tengo dos calculadoras y muchas gomas de borrar. También tengo un diccionario en mi mochila.

Answers (40 points total)

A. School Supplies (10 points: 2 points per item)
1. no   4. sí
2. no   5. sí
3. sí

B. Telling Time (9 points: 3 points per item)
1. c
2. a
3. b

C. School Subjects (14 points: 2 points per item)
1. e   5. d
2. a   6. g
3. c   7. b
4. f

D. Days of the Week (5 points)
8. **jóvenes** is not a day of the week.

E. ¿Qué día es? (2 points)
7. lunes, (Monday is the first day of the week)

Scripts and Answers for ¡Ya lo sé!, Units 4 and 5

Unit 4 ¡Ya lo sé!

Script
A. Sports and Free-time Activities
1. Sí, me gustaría escuchar la música rock después de las clases.
2. Sí, me gustaría montar en bicicleta con Carmen.
3. Sí, me gustaría jugar al fútbol mañana.
4. Sí, me gustaría practicar el piano después de las clases.
5. Sí, me gustaría estudiar después de las clases.

Answers (40 points total)
A. Invitations (10 points: 2 points per item)
1. c
2. a
3. b
4. e
5. d

B. El Paseo (8 points: 4 points per item)
1. b
2. c

C. Pastimes (10 points: 2 points per item)
1. c
2. a
3. e
4. d
5. b

D. Opinions (12 points: 3 points per item)
Answers will vary. Possible answers:
1. Sí, me gusta nadar porque es divertido.
2. Sí, me gusta estudiar porque es interesante.
3. Sí, me gusta jugar a los videojuegos porque es fácil.
4. No, no me gusta hablar por teléfono porque es aburrido.

Unit 5 ¡Ya lo sé!

Script
A. Weather
1. Hace mucho frío en Nueva York en el invierno.
2. Hace mucho sol en Miami durante el verano.
3. Hace fresco en Portland en la primavera.
4. Es otoño y hace viento en Chicago.

Answers (40 points total)
A. Seasons (8 points: 2 points per item)
1. d   2. b   3. a   4. c

B. Holidays (10 points: 2 points per item)
1. a
2. d
3. c
4. e
5. b

C. Sports
(16 points: 4 points per item)
1. esquío
2. patino en línea
3. nado
4. juego al fútbol

D. Las fechas (6 points: 3 points per item)
1. c
2. b

Unit 6 ¡Ya lo sé!

Script

A. Breakfast

LUISA	Roberto, ¿Te gusta comer cereal para el desayuno?
ROBERTO	Me gusta más comer los huevos con tocino. ¿Y tú?
LUISA	Me gusta el pan tostado. Para beber, me gusta la leche.
ROBERTO	Para beber, me gusta el jugo de naranja.

Answers (40 points total)

A. Breakfast (10 points: 2 points per item)
1. Luisa
2. Roberto
3. Roberto
4. Luisa
5. Roberto

B. Lunch (12 points: 4 points per item)
1. c
2. a
3. b

C. Dinner at the Restaurant
(14 points: 2 points per item)
1. b   5. d
2. a   6. h
3. g   7. f
4. e

D. La comida (4 points: 2 points per item)
1. cierto
2. falso

Unit 7 ¡Ya lo sé!

Script

A. Where are you going?
— Hola, Georgina. ¿Adónde vas?
— Hola, Jorge. Voy al gimnasio. ¿Y tú, adónde vas?
— Voy al restaurante y por la noche voy al cine.
— Muy bien. Yo voy al cine mañana. Adiós, Jorge.
— Hasta luego, Georgina.

Answers (40 points total)

A. Where are you going?
(8 points: 4 points per item)
1. **Georgina:** d, c
2. **Jorge:** b, c

B. Animals (12 points: 2 points per item)
1. e
2. b
3. a
4. f
5. c
6. d

C. Directions (12 points: 3 points per item)
1. e
2. d
3. c
4. a

D. Los Parques Nacionales (8 points: 4 points per item)
1. c, e
2. b

SCRIPTS AND ANSWERS

Unit 8 ¡Ya lo sé!

Script
A. Family
1. Laura es mi hermana.
2. Jaime es mi abuelo.
3 Rosa es mi madre.
4. Luisa es mi abuela.
5 Julio es mi padre.
6. Mario es mi hermano.

Answers (40 points total)
A. Family (12 points: 2 points per item)
1. sí
2. no
3. sí
4. sí
5. sí
6. no

B. Introductions (12 points: 3 points per item)
1. FEDERICO **Ésta es** mi amiga Luisa.
   TEODORO Mucho gusto Luisa.
2. LUISA **¿Cómo te llamas?**
3. TEODORO **Me llamo** Teodoro.
4. LUISA **Mucho gusto,** Teodoro.

C. Descriptions (10 points: 2 points per item)
1. e
2. c
3. b
4. a
5. d

D. Saludos (6 points: 2 points per item)
1. c
2. a
3. b

Unit 9 ¡Ya lo sé!

Script
A. The Body
1. la pierna
2. la nariz
3. la mano
4. el ojo
5. el brazo
6. los dedos
7. el oído
8. el estómago

Answers (40 points total)
A. The Body (16 points: 2 points per item)
1. h
2. c
3. d
4. a
5. e
6. f
7. b
8. g

B. Clothing (12 points: 2 points per item)
1. b
2. a
3. b
4. d
5. c
6. c

C. Shopping (8 points: 2 points each)
1. a, c
2. b, d

D. La cultura (4 points: 2 points per item)
1. falso
2. cierto